JN435108

Intermediate Academic English

College English

SECOND EDITION

Reading and Writing

Robert Jeens

YONSEI UNIVERSITY PRESS

SECOND EDITION

College English

Intermediate Academic English

Reading and Writing

Robert Jeens

Copyright©2010 by the Yonsei University Press
All rights reserved.

262 Seongsanno, Seodaemun-gu, Seoul 120-749, Korea
TEL: (82-2) 2123-3380~2
FAX: (82-2) 2123-8673
E-mail: ysup@yonsei.ac.kr
http://www.yonsei.ac.kr/press

ISBN 978-89-7141-914-4 (93740)

Price ₩15,000

Forward

I would like to thank the people who made this book possible. First, I'd like to thank my colleagues at Yonsei University. Their insights into teaching methods and helpful suggestions were crucial to my evolution as a teacher and a materials developer. To Duane Henning: thanks for helping me with my computer questions. To everyone else: thanks for your support. Second, I'd like to thank my students. They were my guinea pigs. There was no better judge of the worthiness of my materials, or lack thereof. Third, I'd like to thank the administration at University College and in the English Education Committee. All too often, in the quest to keep standards of teaching up, control is enforced and unifomity leads to mediocrity. The fact that we are allowed to bring our ideas to fruition is largely due to them. Lastly, I'd like to thank my wife. She put up with my hours at the computer, lost Sundays and various other instances of neglect. She is my most valuable companion.

IIITo the teachers who use this book: do not take this book as a whole document that must be followed page-by-page. While I developed it to be progressive in difficulty and possible to teach with little preparation, the quality of the materials in it can be greatly enhanced by a little imagination and preparation. Cut up the reading passages and use them as information-gap activities. Use the grammar activities to make games and jigsaws. Time activities to push your students. Choose the parts of the book most interesting and useful to you and your students. Teaching language is about two things: knowledge about language and knowledge about how-to-teach. Engaging students in the endeavor is always worthwhile, and if you customize this book so that you personally believe in the value of what you are doing, your enthusiasm and effort will be appreciated by your students.

Introduction

This is an academic reading and writing book intended for general Freshman students at universities in Korea. Korean Freshman courses are currently moving away from "English for no Specific Reason" towards "English for Academic Purposes." Yonsei is at the forefront of that revolution, and this book was developed with this in mind. Teachers will want to use this book because the reading topics will interest their students, the grammar is useful for common problems that Korean students have, and because the rhetorical modes are common in academic writing.

The reading and writing format of this book is meant to be complementary, so that the strategies developed in one skill can be transferred to the other. The reading activities are meant to provide introductions to the writing activities, and to provide examples from which students can incorporate techniques useful to their writing. In contrast to the sentence building, from simple-to-complex method used to develop sentences in the writing section, the reading activities provide holistic, real-world examples of English writing. The academic writing activities move from paragraphs to essays in a formatted, planned, and formal manner. On the other hand, the reaction writing activities do not utilize isolated sentences, but draw examples from where they naturally occur, and give students opportunities to practice their writing in context.

Another notable feature of this book is the use of the Academic Word List, as developed by Averil Coxhead. Every use of these words in the book has been highlighted so that students can become aware of the natural usages of these words. Besides that, a word-building activity occurs in every chapter in which students must manipulate the form of the words. Finally, theVre is an appendix at the back of the book in which all the words in the list, in all their forms, has been recorded. Obviously, many other activities could be developed by the teacher from this base.

Table of Contents

Chapter 3 The Final Frontier • 35

Chapter 4 Korean Geography • 59

Chapter 5 Scientific Controversies • 79

Chapter 6 Korean Education • 101

Chapter

01 Medical Advances

Introducing the **Topic**

Student A

Look at the picture on the right and try to describe it to your **partner**.

Student B

Turn to page 6.

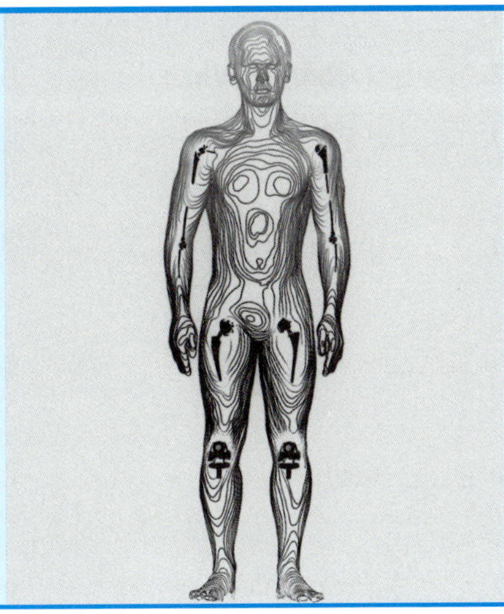

Reading Strategy — Main Ideas and Important Details

When you read a passage, it is useful to look first for main ideas and then again for details. Try this **method**. First, scan any pictures, **charts** or subtitles. Then read quickly through the main **text**. Do not stop to use your dictionary or worry about the meaning of unknown words. When you are finished, write down what you think are the most important ideas. At this point, if there are any comprehension questions after the reading passage, read them and keep them in mind while you are reading. Next, read through the passage carefully, using your dictionary if necessary. Answer the questions. **Finally**, read the passage one more time to check your answers.

Focus Question

Do you think it is possible for people to regenerate missing limbs or organs?

Task 1-1 Vocabulary

Match the words on the left with their **definitions** on the right.

1. _____ a bypass operation
2. _____ a diabetic ulcer
3. _____ a limb
4. _____ an organ
5. _____ scaffolding
6. _____ tissue
7. _____ a transplant

a) arm or leg
b) for example, heart, liver, lung, or kidney
c) an operation in which a new organ is put into someone's body
d) a **structure** around which something can be built
e) a group of cells in an animal which are **similar** and have the same purpose
f) a large open sore on the body caused by diabetes
g) an operation to change the flow of blood to avoid a diseased part of someone' heart

Finding the **Main Ideas**

Task 1-2 Skimming

Here is a useful activity to help you **identify** the main ideas. Below is a list of subtitles for the reading passage below. Quickly read the passage and put the subtitles in the correct spaces in the **text.**

a) Heart Regeneration
b) Limb Regeneration
c) Skin Regeneration
d) The Limits of Modern **Medicine**
e) What is Regenerative **Medicine**?

Recent Advances in Regenerative **Medicine**

Consider the following examples. A young girl was in a serious car accident and lost her leg. Fortunately, doctors and scientists now have the ability to replace her leg with an artificial one so that she can lead a **normal** life. **Alternatively**, a young man had a seriously damaged heart. He **underwent** a heart transplant, which added years to his life. **Finally**, a firefighter is seriously burned. Months of skin grafts and other treatments have allowed him to **survive**. These are three examples of how modern **medical technology** has improved people's lives.

1. ______________________________

Modern **medical procedures** have extended and improved the **quality** of life for millions of people all over the world, yet the people above may not enjoy a full **recovery**. While artificial limbs are better than no limbs at all, the user faces some limitations in **function** and look. Unfortunately, after an organ transplant, the patient's body may **reject** the transplanted organ **despite** the use of anti-**rejection** drugs, which may have serious side-effects. The firefighter in question, although healed, may be seriously scarred. In all these situations, there are **maintenance issues** that will have to be addressed for years to come.

2. ______________________________

Some **medical researchers** are looking for answers to these problems in the field of regenerative **medicine**. For these **researchers**, the solution is to grow a new leg, a new heart or new skin. Instead of continually treating the symptoms of a disease, regenerative **medicine practitioners** want to permanently return the body of the patient back to the state it was in before the damage **occurred** by **utilizing** regenerating **techniques**. While this may seem unbelievable to some, recent advances have given new hope to people suffering from **similar** conditions.

3. ______________________________

Limb regeneration is an old idea into which new research is being done. Scientists have long known that creatures like newts and salamanders can regenerate lost legs or tails, and babies under the age of about 5 can regenerate fingertips. **Utilizing** this **principle**, if it is possible to replace part of a toe, why not a whole leg? Would this work on **adult** humans? Stephen Badylak and his **team** at the University of Pittsburg have used specially-treated tissue **derived** from pigs to regenerate damaged tissue in humans and other animals. This **research** has had great success, healing diabetic ulcers and other **previously** untreatable wounds in over 400,000 patients around the world. Recently, Badylak's **team** regenerated a fingertip in a 78 year-old-man. They have now been given a **grant** to **evaluate** the application of this process in the regeneration of full limbs. Badylak or someone like him may make a breakthrough soon.

4. ______________________________

Previously, there had been no way to repair damaged hearts, but that is changing. Doctors could give heart attack patients bypass surgery to repair damaged arteries leading to the heart, but the damage in the heart muscle itself remained permanent. This led, in many patients, to either death or the need for a heart transplant. A new **treatment**, pioneered by Dr. Amit Patel at the Center for Cardiac Therapy, uses stem cells taken from the patient, which are injected directly into the heart. These start the repair of the damaged tissue, so that a heart transplant is no longer necessary. How about growing a whole new heart? Taru Akanu at Tokyo Women's Hospital has already grown beating heart muscle in a Petri dish. At the same time as these **teams pursue**

regenerating our hearts, other teams are working on regenerating skin.

5. ______________________________

Skin regeneration offers new hope for severe burn victims. The **conventional** treatment has been to graft **uninjured** skin from another part of the body of the victim onto the **injury**. Unfortunately, in severe burn patients, there is often not enough **uninjured** skin to transplant, and there is a great danger of infection. Now a new cell "seeding" **technique** offers the possibility of regenerating healthy skin. **A** bio-**reactor** "gun" sprays new cells into the wound, fertilizing the **environment** so that infection is **inhibited** and the growth of new skin encouraged. There is little scarring: the healed wound looks natural. Other **teams** are developing a "scaffolding" **approach** to growing new ears and noses to reattach onto patients with severe facial burns. Doctors wish to **establish** whether it may be possible to completely **reconstruct** extremely damaged faces.

The **techniques** discussed are at different stages of development. What they have in common is that they are costly and **require** large numbers of specialists to develop and **implement**. The good news is regenerative medicine is receiving some serious **funding** from, among others, the Japanese government and the U.S. **military**, which is looking for better ways to treat wounded soldiers. Regenerating parts of our bodies may not be **exclusively** the preserve of reptiles, fish or science fiction much longer.

Introducing the **Topic**

Student B

Look at the picture on the right and try to describe it to your **partner**.

Student A

Turn to page 1.

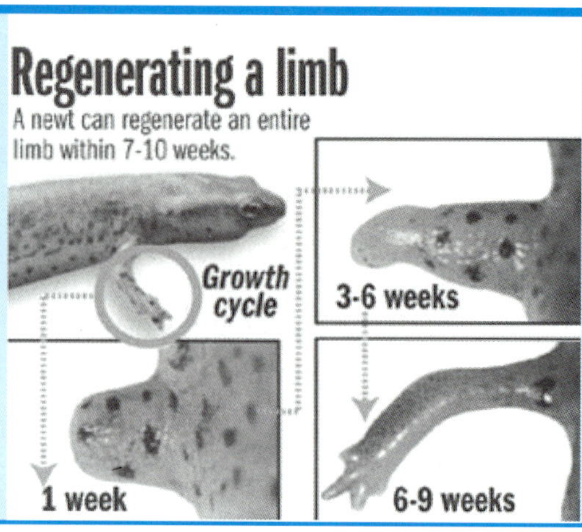

Reading Strategy — Problem-Solution

This article is an example of a problem-solution composition, in which the **author** sets up a "problem" to which he offers a solution. The problem-solution composition is one of the most effective and common **structures** you will **encounter**.

Task 1-3

Read the article again. Fill in the diagram below to see how the **structure** of this problem-solution essay works. Check your answers with a **partner**

Main Problem	⇨	Main Solution
Example Problem #1	⇨	Example Solution #1

Example Problem #2	→	Example Solution #2
Example Problem #3	→	Example Solution #3

Comprehension Questions

Task 1-4

1. What are the dangers of **conventional** organ transplant, as related in the article?

2. What is the main purpose of regenerative **medicine**?

3. Which animals can regenerate lost limbs?

4. What exactly has Steven Badylak's **team** been doing?

5. What two **methods** of regenerating heart tissue are discussed?

6. What is the problem with **conventional methods** of treating severe burns?

7. How does the bioreactor gun work?

8. Who is providing more money for research?

9. What is the tone of the article?

   a) happy   b) pessimistic   c) optimistic   d) authoritative

Reacting to the Article

Task 1-5

Discuss the following questions with a **partner**.

1. How would your life change if you lost an arm or a leg, or became blind or deaf?

2. Do you think that doctors and scientists will ever be able to grow new limbs or organs for people? If no, why not? If yes, what are the **implications** of this for human lifespan and lifestyle?

3. How would the world be different if no one ever died, or if our life spans were **expanded** greatly?

4. Write one more question that you would like to ask your **partner** about the **topic**.

   ▶ ______________________________

5. Write about 150 words on one of the **topics** above. Include five words from the **Academic** Word List, **highlighted** in bold.

Writing Strategy — The Parts of the Paragraph

There are three parts to a **paragraph** – the **topic** sentence, the body and the **concluding** sentence.

The Title of a Paragraph

Task 1- 6

1. Underline the title of this **chapter**.
2. Underline the title of the example **paragraph.**

Although not a part of the paragraph, titles help writers to begin to **focus** on the subject of their writing. It gives the reader a clue as to what will be in the story. Sometimes the title is only one word, such as *Spiderman* or *Titanic*. A good title catches the reader's interest, but it does not have to tell everything about the **paragraph**.

Example Paragraph : Paragraph Form

Date

Your Name and Student Number

Instructor's Name

title centered

The Human Genome **Project**

indent first line

12-point type

The Human Genome **Project** was an excellent example of modern, "big" science that transcended boundaries and has had earth-changing ramifications. The **project sought** to determine the **sequence** of **chemical** base pairs which **comprise** DNA and to **identify** how the **approximately** 25,000 genes of the human genome both were ordered and **functioned**. In addition to the United States, the international consortium was **comprised** of geneticists in China, France, Germany, Japan and the United Kingdom. Most of the **research** was **conducted** in universities and **research** centers in the United States, Canada and Britain. Although the **project** was slated to continue for 15 years, due to advances in **sequence analysis** and **computing technology**, a "rough **draft**" of the genome was finished in 2000. **Ongoing analysis** led to the complete genome being announced and made **available** on the Internet in 2003. This knowledge has already led to advances in **medicine** and biotechnology, and the **potential benefits** may be almost limitless.

Do not begin new sentences on new lines

left margin

right margin

double-spaced

The **Topic** Sentence

Task 1-7

1. Underline the **topic** sentence of the example **paragraph**.
2. Underline the **topic** sentences in the paragraphs in the reading passage, *Recent Advances in Regenerative* ***Medicine***.
3. Compare your choices with a **partner**. Do you agree or disagree? Why or why not?

Here are some rules for finding and writing topic sentences.

1. The **topic** sentence is usually the first sentence of a **paragraph**.
2. The **topic** sentence relates to every sentence in a **paragraph**. When you read the **topic** sentence, you should know what the **paragraph** is about.
3. A good **topic** sentence is something that can be **demonstrated** or has to be proved to be true. *There are many Koreans in Korea* is true, but not a good **topic** sentence because everyone knows it is true.
4. A good **topic** sentence has a controlling idea. The controlling idea narrows the flow of ideas in the **paragraph**.

Topic Sentence	Topic	Controlling Idea
Limb regeneration is an old idea becoming new again.	Limb regeneration	is an old idea into which new research is being done.
Previously, there had been no way to repair damaged hearts, but that is changing.	damaged hearts	**Previously**, there had been no way to repair …, but that is changing.
The Human Genome Project was an excellent example of modern, "big" science that transcended boundaries and has had earth-changing ramifications.	The Human Genome Project	was an excellent example of modern, "big" science that transcended boundaries and has had earth-changing ramifications.

Task 1-8

1. Circle the **topic** and underline the controlling ideas in sentences a), b) and c).
2. Choose the best **topic** sentence for the following **paragraph**.

The Smallpox Vaccine

a) Dr. Edward Jenner was born in England in 1749.
b) Dr Edward Jenner invented the vaccination against smallpox in 1796.
c) Dr. Edward Jenner pioneered one of the most important **techniques** in modern **medicine**.

____

Dr Jenner was **aware** that many farmers who had been **exposed** to cowpox, a **similar** disease **found** in cows, never developed smallpox. He also knew that in Eastern Asia, people were inoculated with matter **acquired** from people who had a mild case of smallpox. The problem with the second **method** was that about 2% of people so inoculated died from the disease. In a first for modern medicine, he therefore inoculated an 8-year-old boy infected with smallpox with matter **obtained** from a cowpox pustule. The boy quickly **recovered**. Millions of people around the world **subsequently benefited** from Dr. Jenner's discovery, which led to the modern science of inoculation against disease. In 1802, Dr. Jenner was awarded 10,000 pounds sterling from the British parliament in recognition of his work.

The Body of the **Paragraph**

The main part of the **paragraph** is called the body. It is here that the idea presented in the **topic** sentence will be developed. If a **paragraph** does not have a good body, readers will not be able to follow the ideas. The **paragraph** may be confusing or **illogical**.

Two common problems with the bodies of **paragraphs** are redundancy and **relevance**. Redundancy is very common and **somewhat** of a problem, while **relevance** is perhaps less common, but a very serious mistake.

Redundancy

Redundant means *not needed* or *more than necessary*. In the sentence, "*He lives together with his family*," the word "*together*" is redundant. It just repeats the idea of "*with his family*." Also, if you say something in one sentence, and then say it again in another sentence, one of the sentences is redundant.

This is a very common mistake because students often think that if something is important, they should repeat it. We do this in speaking. In writing, however, rather than repeating important information, within a paragraph. you should give an example or explanation of an important point.

Task 1- 9

Underline the two redundant sentences in the **paragraph** below.

Penicillin: The Real Story

Although the story of the accidental discovery of penicillin by Alexander Fleming in 1928 is well-known, it took another 15 years and work by many other **researchers** to **finally** realize the full **potential** of the first modern antibiotic. Fleming understood the **implications** of his discovery but he had trouble **isolating** the antibiotic agent and producing penicillin in quantity. Alexander Fleming did not **solely** develop penicillin. By 1939, Dr. Howard Florey and Ernest Chain at Oxford University had **isolated** and **concentrated** penicillin; however, they could not produce it in the mass quantities necessary for it to become a widely **available** cure. Unfortunately, they could not make enough. In 1941, Florey and Norman Heatley went to Peoria Lab the US to **seek** help. By 1943, Andrew Moyer, Peoria lab's **expert** on the nutrition of molds, had managed to increase the yield of penicillin 10 times. This made mass production possible, so drug companies began manufacturing penicillin, especially for the treatment of **injured** Allied soldiers.

Relevance

A **paragraph** needs unity. This means that everything in the **paragraph** must relate back to the **topic** sentence. Sometimes the writer goes astray and begins writing about things that are not covered in the **topic** sentence. *All the sentences in a* ***paragraph*** *must be* ***relevant****; that is, they must be about the same subject as the* ***topic*** *sentence.*

Task 1- 10

1. Identify the topic sentences in the **paragraphs** below.
2. For each of the underlined sentences, write ***relevant*** *sentence or* ***irrelevant*** *sentence* on the lines below the **paragraph**. One sentence is **irrelevant**.

Cancer Vaccines: Problems and **Prospects**

1. Cancer is **widespread**: in 2007, over 550,000 Americans died of cancer. Human immune systems are vulnerable to cancer because they do not recognize tumors as dangerous or foreign, and thus do not mount a strong attack against them. 2. Tumor cells are **derived** from **normal** cells, so that tumor molecules do not arouse an effective immune **response**. Therefore, although there are many molecular **dissimilarities** between **normal** cells and tumor cells, cancer cells are not truly foreign to the body. 3. They are **normal** molecules, either **altered** in subtle ways or more abundant. This fact will make **researchers'** efforts to make effective cancer vaccines much more **challenging**.

1. ______________________
2. ______________________
3. ______________________

Types of Cancer Vaccine

There are two possible types of cancer vaccines: those that prevent the development of cancer and those that treat existing cancer. 1) Some cancers, such as cervical cancer and some liver cancers, are caused by viruses, and **traditional** vaccines against those viruses, such as HPV vaccine and Hepatitis B vaccine, will prevent those cancers. Scientists have also been trying to develop vaccines against existing cancers. 2) Some **researchers** believe that cancer cells routinely arise and are destroyed by the healthy immune system; cancer forms when the immune system fails to destroy them. 3) Such therapeutic cancer vaccines are being developed for the treatment of breast, lung, colon, skin, kidney, prostate, and other cancers. In **conclusion**, vaccines either try to **constrain** or **neutralize** cancers.

1. ____________________
2. ____________________
3. ____________________

The **Concluding** Sentence

A **concluding** sentence shows that the writer has completed what she wants to say and leaves a strong, **final** statement in the reader's mind. To write effective **concluding** sentences, follow these rules.

1. There is only one **concluding** sentence in any **paragraph**.
2. Do not introduce new ideas in the **concluding** sentence.
3. A **concluding** sentence may **utilize** one of the following **techniques**.
   a) It may *summarize* the **paragraph** by restating the **topic** sentence in different words.
   b) It may state a *conclusion* to the **paragraph** by bringing together the details into a kind of unity.

c) It may *offer a solution* to the problem stated in the **paragraph**.

d) It may **illustrate** *the end of a* ***process***, without introducing a new step in the **process**.

e) It may *make a* ***prediction*** about something that will result from the situation described in the **paragraph**.

Task 1- 11

Look back at the **paragraphs** on pages 9 to 14.

1. Underline the **concluding** sentences.
2. Which of the **techniques** above does the **author** use in the concluding sentences?
3. Work with a **partner** and check your answers.

Task 1- 12

Write a title, **topic** sentence and **concluding** sentence for each of the following groups of sentences.

1.

____

____

____

According to germ **theory**, a **specific** disease is caused by a **specific** organism. Before this discovery, most doctors believed diseases were caused by spontaneous **generation** or bad air. In fact, doctors would perform autopsies on people who died of infectious diseases and then care for living patients without washing their hands, not realizing that they were therefore **transmitting** the disease. During the second half of the 19th century, scientists such as Louis Pasteur, Robert Koch, and Joseph Lister proved that these practices were killing people and **advocated** and developed germ **theory**, leading to antibiotics and antiseptic practices in surgery.

____

____

2. ______________________________

____

____

Before this important discovery, scientists and doctors knew that mixing blood from two **individuals** could lead to blood clumping. These clumped red cells could crack and cause toxic **reactions**, leading to fatal **consequences**. However, Dr. Karl Landsteiner discovered that blood clumping was an immunological **reaction** which **occurs** when the receiver of a blood transfusion has a different blood type than that of the donor. Dr. Landsteiner's work paved the way for blood transfusions to be carried out safely. He was given **credit** for this discovery and awarded the 1930 Nobel Prize for developing the ABO system of blood typing.

____

____

Sentence Building: What is a Sentence?

Definition

A *sentence* is a group of words that contains a subject and a verb and can stand alone as a complete thought.

These are sentences

1. This knowledge has already led to advances.
2. **Consider** the following examples.
3. Would this work on **adult** humans?
4. Yes, I am.
5. These clumped red cells could crack.

These are not sentences

1. An international effort.
2. Offers new hope.
3. They **normal** molecules.
4. Although highly **controversial** when first proposed.
5. This **research** has had.

Sentence Fragments

A sentence fragment is a part of a sentence or a piece of a sentence. It is not a whole sentence.

Sentence Fragments	Why?	Correction
An international effort.	• needs a subject and a verb	The Human Genome **Project** was an international effort.
Offers new hope.	• no subject	Skin regeneration offers new hope.
They **normal** molecules.	• no verb	They are **normal** molecules.
Although highly **controversial** when first proposed	• not a complete thought	Although highly **controversial** when first proposed, germ **theory** is now the cornerstone of modern **medicine** and microbiology.
This **research** has had.	• not a complete thought	This **research** has had great success.

Task 1- 13

Decide which groups of words are sentences and which are sentence fragments. Write *S* next to the *sentences* and *FRAG* next to the *sentence fragments*. Correct the sentence fragments to make sentences.

1. _____ Soldiers from World War I and II with facial injuries and burns were among the first to benefit from plastic surgery.

   ▶ ____

2. _____ Later, these techniques were.

   ▶ ____

3._____ Reconstructive surgery deformed people a normal appearance.

⊙____

4. _____ Cosmetic surgery is concerned with enhancing one's appearance towards some ideal.

⊙____

5. _____ Before reconstructive surgery became common, stared at and often cruelly treated.

⊙____

6. _____ Although cosmetic surgery has allowed people to increase their self-esteem.5

⊙____

7. _____ Afterward, patients' confidence and energy.

⊙____

8. _____ Because some plastic surgery doctors are unqualified.

⊙____

9. _____ The government is considering more heavily regulating the industry.

⊙____

10. _____ Want plastic surgery?

⊙____

Academic Vocabulary Development

The vocabulary **highlighted** in bold type in this book comes from the **Academic** Word List. The **Academic** Word List contains the 570 most commonly used words in **academic** English. For a complete list of the different forms of all the words in the **Academic** Word List, see **Appendix 3**.

Task 1- 14

Adjectives

You must put the word that follows the sentence into its correct adjectival form and use it to fill in the blank in the sentence. Check these sentences with the original sentences from the **text** to see how different forms of the word are used.

1. The ____________ thing to do is read the passage one more time to check your answers. **(finally) (1)**

2. Doctors and scientists now have the ability to replace her leg with an artificial one so that she can lead a ____________ life. **(normal) (3)**

3. To **consider** an ____________ case, a young man has a seriously damaged heart. **(alternatively) (3)**

4. Modern ____________ **procedures** have extended and improved the **quality** of life for millions all over the world, yet the people above may never be fully ____________. **(medicine, recovery) (3)**

5. Stephen Badylak and his **team** at the University of Pittsburg have used specially-treated, pig- ____________tissue to treat and regenerate damaged tissue in humans and other animals. **(derived) (4)**

6. The **conventional** treatment has been to graft **uninjured** skin from another part of the body of the victim onto the ____________ **area. (injury) (5)**

7. The good news is well- ____________ regenerative medicine studies are taking place due to the generosity of, among others, the Japanese government and the U.S. **military. (funding) (5)**

8. Millions of people around the world have enjoyed ____________ results from Dr. Jenner's discovery. **(benefited) (11)**

9. Afterwards, patients are more confident and ____________. **(energy) (18)**

Academic Writing Assignment: The Paragraph

Write a one-**paragraph** composition on the following **topic**: which of the **medical** advances presented in this **chapter** is the most important? In your **paragraph**, you must use at least five words from the **Academic** Word List that have appeared in this **chapter**. Type the words in bold so that your teacher can easily identify them.

Whenever you write, you should go through a four-step **process**: planning, **drafting**, editing, and a **final draft**. Effective writers do all of these, often returning to their words time and again until they have a polished composition. Below is one possible way to write a **focused** and well-ordered **paragraph**.

The Writing Process

1. Planning: Clustering The first thing you need to do is decide which **medical** advance presented in this **chapter** is the most important. To do this, read over the **selections**. If you still can't decide, look at the top two or three and write them on a blank piece of paper. Circle them. Then begin drawing lines out from them with reasons that you think they are important. Circle them. Draw new lines radiating out from these reasons with support for them. Try to give examples, details, or **logical consequences**. Here is an example.

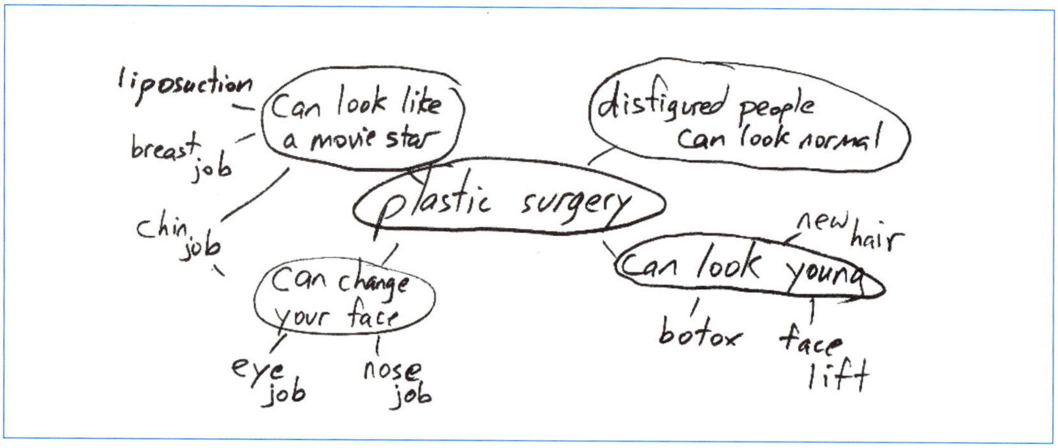

2. Once you have made your cluster of ideas, cross out **irrelevant** or unimportant ideas and try **to expand** the best ideas.

3. Outline In your outline, include a title and **topic** sentence, order your reasons and their supports, and include a concluding sentence. Are your reasons the best you can think of? Do you support your reasons with good evidence such as examples, details or the opinions of experts?

Sample Outline
Title: *The* ***Benefits*** *of Plastic Surgery*
Topic Sentence: *The three most important* ***benefits*** *of plastic surgery are: it can make older people look younger, it can* ***enhance*** *anyone's* ***physical*** *appearance, and it can enable the disfigured to lead a normal life.*
Body: A: First Point: *older people can look younger* 1. **Evidence**: *botox, face lift, hair transplants* B: Second Point: *improve* ***physical*** *appearance* 2. **Evidence**: *nose* ***job****, eye* ***job****, breast* ***job****, liposuction* C: Third Point: *disfigured people can have a normal appearance* 3. *cleft palate,* ***major reconstructive*** *surgery*
Concluding Sentence: *Whether or not you decide to have plastic surgery, it is important to have an informed opinion before you* ***proceed****.*

4. First Draft Next, write your first **draft**. Make sure that your **topic** sentence fits your **paragraph**. Be sure the body has unity: **eliminate irrelevant** or repetitive ideas. The **concluding** sentence should leave the reader with a strong impression.

5. Edit Check your first **draft** against the **paragraph** checklist below. If you find any mistakes, **revise**.

6. Final Draft Hand in an eight-to-twelve-sentence **paragraph** to your teacher.

Medical Advances **Paragraph** Checklist

Form

- Is the **paragraph** typed in 12-point type and double-spaced?
- Is the first line of the paragraph indented?
- Are there 8-12 sentences?
- Does one sentence directly follow the next (don't write new sentences on new lines)?

Organization

- Is there a **topic** sentence with a **topic** and a controlling idea?
- Are all the sentences **relevant**?
- Is there any redundancy?
- Is there an effective **concluding** sentence?

Content

- Does the writer engage the reader's interest in the title and topic sentence?
- Does the writer give reasons for his or her opinion?
- Does the writer support the reasons with **evidence**?
- Are there 5 words from the **Academic** Word List in bold?

Grammar and Mechanics

- Does the writer avoid mistakes of spelling, capitalization and punctuation?
- Are there any mistakes of singular or plural?
- Does the writer avoid sentence fragments?
- Are adjectives used correctly?

Chapter

02 Food Science

Healthy Eating Questionnaire

Student A

Student A, stay here.

Student B go to page 24.

First, fill in the answers to the questions below.

Next, ask your **partner** the questions and write in his or her answers.

Finally, compare your answers. Who is the healthiest eater?

Are you a healthy eater?

	You	Your **partner**
1. Do you eat 3 meals a day?		
always	☐	☐
sometimes	☐	☐
never	☐	☐
2. How often do you eat fruits and vegetables?		
2 or 3 times a day	☐	☐
once a day	☐	☐
never	☐	☐
3. How often do you eat meat?		
2 or 3 times a week	☐	☐
every day	☐	☐
every meal	☐	☐
4. Do you eat late night snacks?		
every day	☐	☐
sometimes	☐	☐
never	☐	☐
5. How often do you drink alcohol?		
3 times a week	☐	☐
once or twice a week	☐	☐
never	☐	☐

Healthy Eating Questionnaire

Student B

Student B, stay here.

Student A go to page 23.

First, fill in the answers to the questions below.

Next, ask your **partner** the questions and write in his or her answers.

Finally, compare your answers. Who is the healthiest eater?

Are you a healthy eater?

	You	Your **partner**
1. Do you love pizza, hamburgers, and fried chicken?		
yes	☐	☐
no	☐	☐
2. Do you drink cola more often than water?		
yes	☐	☐
no	☐	☐
3. Do you **consider** Sam Gyup Sal a healthy choice?		
yes	☐	☐
no	☐	☐
4. Do you eat whole grain bread, rice or noodles?		
yes	☐	☐
no	☐	☐
5. Do you eat fish at least twice a week?		
yes	☐	☐
no	☐	☐

Reading Strategy | **Prediction**

Task 2-1 Look at the title of the reading passage on the next page. What ingredients do you think could be in the soup? How do you think it could be made? Share your answers with a **partner**.

Task 2-2

Some of the **instructions** in the reading passage are out of order. Put them in order and number all the **instructions**.

My Mom's Italian Vegetable Soup

Before I left home for university, my mother decided I had to know how to cook a few simple dishes. She knew I would be living alone, worried about it, and told me I needed to learn to cook for myself or eat at Macdonald's. Well, I hate Big Macs, so my mom taught me how to cook. Fortunately, this has led me to a life-long **devotion** to cooking.

Over the years, I have learned how to cook many delicious dishes, but a few of the meals that my mother taught me are still among my favorites. I make them, from time to time, for my friends and family, and most people enjoy them. Try the one below, and maybe you will, too.

Ingredients

1 **medium** onion	2 stalks of celery	15 ml oregano
2 **medium** potatoes	1 **medium** zucchini	30 ml olive oil
1 can of tomatoes	1/2 can of spaghetti sauce	5 ml of black pepper
4 cloves of garlic	1 can corn	15 ml of basil
1 large carrot	1 1/2 liters of water	3 cubes chicken stock

Instructions

_____ After you have begun to cook the vegetables, crush the garlic cloves and add them to the pot.

_____ Stir the vegetables over the heat with the olive oil for 10 minutes to seal in the flavor.

_____ Pour the olive oil over the vegetables and turn on the burner.

_____ While the vegetables are cooking in the pot, add the corn, tomatoes, spaghetti sauce, water, basil, oregano, chicken stock, and black pepper to the pot.

_____ After adding the water and other ingredients, heat on high until the soup boils.

_____ First, chop up the onion, celery, carrot, potato and zucchini into cubes and place them in a large soup pot.

_____ Turn down the heat and let the soup simmer for one hour, stirring occasionally.

_____ Serve with garlic bread.

This makes about 10 servings of soup. You have two **options**. You could invite some friends over to share it with you, or you might want to wait until it cools down and freeze it in **individual** servings, so that you can eat it later. It's up to you. Enjoy.

Reading Grammar: Verb **Tense** Review

Task 2-3

Underline the main verbs in the sentences in number one, and match them with the descriptions in number two.

1. a) Before I left home for university, my mother decided I had to know how to cook a few simple dishes.
   b) Fortunately, this has led me to a life-long love of cooking.
   c) I make them, from time to time, for my friends and family, and everybody enjoys them.
   d) Chop up the onion, celery, carrot, potato and zucchini into cubes and place them in a large soup pot.
   e) The vegetables are cooking in the pot.

2. a) __d__ This verb **tense** is used to give **instructions**.
   b) _____ This verb **tense** is used to describe something that **occurs** repeatedly in the past, present and future.
   c) _____ This verb **tense** is used to describe something happening **temporarily**.
   d) _____ This verb **tense** is used to describe an **incident** that **occurred** at a **definite** time in the past.
   e) _____ This verb tense is used to describe an action in the past that has an **impact** on the present.

3. Match the sentences and descriptions in numbers one and two with the names of the verb **tense** below.
   1. The Imperative **Tense** __1d__ __2a__
   2. The Simple Present **Tense** _____ _____
   3. The Present Continuous **Tense** _____ _____
   4. The Simple Past **Tense** _____ _____
   5. The Present Perfect **Tense** _____ _____

Comprehension Questions

Task 2-4

1. What is the main idea of this writing passage?
   a) how to cook vegetable soup
   b) entering university
   c) eating with your friends
   d) how my mother helped me prepare for life
2. Why did the **author**'s mother teach him to cook?
3. Why did the **author** decide to learn to cook?
4. What was the result of his mother's teachings?
5. Why should you stir the vegetables over heat in olive oil?
6. How much soup does this recipe make?
7. What choice does the **author** give you?

Reaction Questions

Task 2-5

Discuss the following questions with a **partner**.

1. Do you think the soup above would be delicious? Why or why not?
2. Are you or would you like to be a good cook?
3. Tell your **partner** a recipe for a food you can make.
4. Write one more question that you would like to ask your **partner** about the **topic**.

   ____

5. Write 100 to 150 words on the following **topic**: Are you a healthy eater? Include five words from the **Academic** Word List, **highlighted** in bold.

Writing Strategy | Process Analysis

Example Paragraph

Kimchee Chiggae

Kimchee Chiggae is the most basic Korean food that there is, and it is surprisingly easy to make. First, cut up 500 grams of lean pork into bite-sized chunks. Next, in a saucepan, combine the pork with about 500 grams of kimchee, cut into bite-sized chunks, 10 grams of soy sauce, 100 grams of water, 10 grams of crushed red hot peppers, 2 cloves crushed garlic, and a little salt and pepper. Bring it to a boil. After that, turn the heat down to **medium** and simmer until the kimchee is tender. **Finally**, serve **accompanied** with sticky rice. No matter where you are in the world when you eat this, you will taste a little piece of Korea.

Process Analysis Organization

A **process analysis** tells how-to-do something. It begins with a topic sentence, which has a topic and a controlling idea. In the body, divide the **process** into a **series** of steps that your reader can easily follow, then list or explain the steps in time order. Special time words or phrases allow you to tell the reader when a particular step **occurs**. It ends with a **specific** result: you have accomplished something at the end of the **process**.

Task 2-6

Read the example process analysis paragraph, "Kimchee Chigae," fill in the outline below, and then compare your answer with a **partner.**

Title

Topic Sentence

Body

Step 1 ______________________________

Step 2 ______________________________

Step 3 ______________________________

Step 4 ______________________________

Step 5 ______________________________

Concluding Sentence

Sentence Building: **Coordinating** Conjunctions

We use **coordinating** conjunctions to join two sentences together into one sentence.

- Kimchee Chiggae is the most basic Korean food that there is.
- It is surprisingly easy to make.
- Kimchee Chiggae is the most basic Korean food that there is, *and* it is surprisingly easy to make.

When we join two sentences together with a **coordinating** conjunction, we must use a comma (,) before the **coordinating** conjunction. The four most important **coordinating** conjunctions are *and*, *but*, *or* and *so*.

Please note that many **consider** it to be a serious **stylistic** infraction to use *and*, *but*, *or*, or *so* to begin sentences in **academic** writing. When beginning sentences, instead of *and*, use *in addition*; rather than *but*, use *however*; write ***alternatively*** instead of *or*; and *therefore* rather than *so*. Only use *and, but, or*, and *so* to join two sentences.

Joining Sentences	Beginning Sentences
and	*in addition*
but	*however*
or	***alternatively***
so	*therefore*

and We use *and* to join two **similar** ideas.	She knew I would be living alone, *and* told me I needed to learn to cook for myself.
or We use *or* to join two choices or **alternatives**	You could invite some friends over to share it with you, *or* you might want to freeze it into individual servings.
so We use *so* to show that a second idea is the result of the first.	I hate Big Macs, *so* my mom taught me how to cook.
but We use *but* to join two sentences with **contrasting** ideas.	I have learned how to cook many delicious dishes, *but* a few of the meals that my mother taught me are still among my favorites.

Task 2-7

Combine the following sentences using *and, but, or* or *so*. There may be more than one correct answer, but changing the **coordinating** conjunction will change the meaning of the sentence. Don't forget to insert a comma before the coordinating conjunction.

1. Gimbap is delicious, healthy and convenient. It is a popular Korean fast food.

   ⊙ ______________________________

2. It is made from steamed white rice. It often includes long strips of pickled turnip, egg, carrots, and spinach.

   ⊙ ______________________________

3. Sometimes tuna and mayonnaise are added to make tuna gimbap. Another popular variation is beef gimbap, which includes hamburger.

   ⊙ ______________________________

4. A scoop of rice is placed on an A4-sized piece of dried seaweed. The rice is spread out along the bottom to the edges of the seaweed.

   ⊙ ______________________________

5. Other ingredients are placed lengthways on top of the rice. Don't put too many ingredients on it. You won't be able to roll it up.

   ⊙ ______________________________

6. Roll the seaweed over the rice into a roll. Then sprinkle sesame seeds on top.

   ⊙ ______________________________

7. Cut the gimbap into bite-sized pieces. Serve with kimchi.

   ⊙ ______________________________

8. Gimbap is easily carried around. It is often eaten during picnics.

▶ ____

Academic Vocabulary Development

Task 2-8 **Verbs**

You must put the word that follows the sentence into its correct verbal form and use it to fill in the blank in the sentence. Check these sentences with the original sentences from the **text** to see how different word forms are used.

1. The **project sought** __________ the **chemical** base pairs which make up DNA. **(sequence) (9)**
2. Most of the **project** __________ in universities and centers in the United States, Canada and Britain. **(research) (9)**
3. An almost complete **version** of the genome __________ in 2000. **(draft) (9)**
4. Tumor cells are **derived** from **normal** cells, so that tumor molecules do not cause our immune system __________ effectively to them. **(response) (13)**
5. In order __________ well, leave the reader with a strong or interesting **final** thought. **(conclusion) (14)**
6. A **concluding** sentence may __________ something. **(prediction) (15)**
7. Before this discovery, most doctors believed diseases could __________ spontaneously or were caused by bad air. **(generation) (15)**
8. Next, __________ with somebody, ask him the questions and write in his answers. **(partner) (23)**
9. We __________ a **process** to tell how-to-do something. **(analysis) (29)**
10. We use *but* __________ ideas in two sentences. **(contrasting) (30)**

Academic Writing Assignment: Process Analysis

Write a one-**paragraph** composition on the following **topic**: write a recipe to a dish you enjoy. Use at least five words from the **Academic** Word List that have appeared in the book so far. Type the words in bold so that your teacher can easily identify them.

The Writing Process

1. Planning: Brainstorming As its name suggests, brainstorming is a storm in your head. The idea is to **generate** as many ideas as possible, as quickly as possible. The first step in brainstorming is to write down a **series** of points about your **topic**. Set a time limit, in this case, say, 10 minutes, and just write as many points as you can. Don't worry about the **quality** of what you are writing. **Concentrate** upon quantity. You will pick out the good ideas later. It takes quite a bit of practice to become good at brainstorming, so don't worry if you find it difficult at first. You will improve later.

2. Once you have brainstormed a list of ideas, cross out **irrelevant** or unimportant ideas and try to **expand** the best ideas.

3. Outline Look at page 29 for an example outline. In your outline, include a title, **topic** sentence, order your recipe in time order and include a **concluding** sentence. In your **topic** sentence, try to answer a question such as, "What does this food represent?" or, "Why would people want to learn this recipe?" In the body of the paragraph, fully and **clearly** explain the step-by-step **process**. In your **conclusion**, leave the reader with a strong or interesting **final** thought.

4. First Draft Next, write your first **draft**. Write in full sentences. Make sure that your **topic** sentence fits your **paragraph**. Be sure the body has unity: **eliminate irrelevant** or repetitive ideas.

5. Editing Check your first **draft** against the **paragraph** checklist below. If you find any mistakes, **revise**.

6. Final Draft Finally, hand in an eight-to-twelve sentence **paragraph** to your teacher.

Process Analysis Paragraph Checklist

Form

- Is the paragraph typed in 12-point type and double-spaced?
- Are there 8 to 12 sentences?
- Is the first line of the paragraph indented?
- Does one sentence directly follow the next (don't write new sentences on new lines)?

Organization

- Is there a **topic** sentence with a **topic** and a controlling idea?
- Are all the sentences **relevant**?
- Is there any redundancy?
- Is there an effective **concluding** sentence?

Content

- Does the writer engage the reader's interest in the title and **topic** sentence?
- Does the writer fully and **clearly** explain the step-by-step **process**?
- Are there five words from the **Academic** Word List in bold?

Grammar and Mechanics

- Does the writer avoid mistakes of spelling, capitalization and punctuation?
- Are there any mistakes of singular or plural?
- Does the writer avoid sentence fragments?
- Are adjectives used correctly?
- Does the writer use correct verb **tenses**?
- Are **coordinating** conjunctions used correctly?

Chapter

03 The **Final** Frontier

Student A

Space Travel Sentence Dictation and Completion

1. Student A, stay here. Student B, go to page 40.
2. You have the first part of five sentences below. Your **partner** has the second part. Read your sentence beginnings so that your **partner** can match them with the ends of the sentences.
3. Listen to your **partner** dictate the sentence ends and write them in where they belong.

---

1. The International Space Station orbits ______________________
2. The most **visible feature** of the truss **structure** ______________________
3. Living accommodations include a toilet with hygiene **facilities**, __________
4. Destiny is the **primary** U.S. ______________________
5. The racks also contain water and oxygen recycling **equipment** that allows the ______________________.

Task 3-1 **Vocabulary**

Match the words on the left with their **definitions** on the right.

1. _____ an airlock
2. _____ a docking port
3. _____ a module
4. _____ orbit
5. _____ pressurized
6. _____ recycle

a) a container which is full of air in an otherwise airless environment

b) one of a set of separate parts that combine to make a whole **structure**

c) a room between two **areas** that have different air pressures

7. _____ rotate

8. _____ a solar **panel**

d) a **device** that changes **energy** from the sun into electricity

e) to spin around a planet or sun

f) to put something through a **process** so that it can be used again

g) to turn in a circle around a fixed point

h) an **area** of a spaceship that can connect to another spaceship

Finding the **Main Ideas :** Labeling a Diagram

Task 3-2

1. What is the picture below?
2. Read the article and fill in the boxes that list the components. Check your answers with a partner.

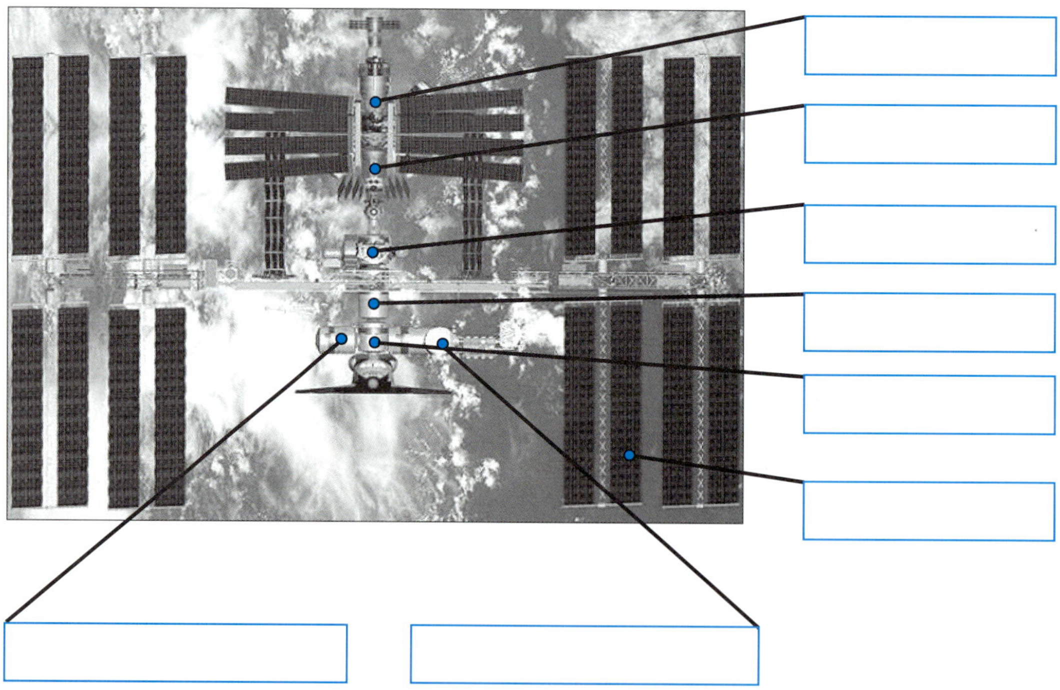

The International Space Station

It hangs, with its wings outstretched, looking like a high-tech **version** of an old-fashioned flying machine. However, this machine does not fly through the air; it orbits 400 kilometers above the earth at 27,700 kilometers per hour. Its **dimension**s are **enormous**, weighing 500 tons and measuring 110 m by 95 m, with a central **core volume** of 1200 m^3. It is the same size as two 747s. **Structurally**, it **consists** of fourteen pressurized modules including laboratories, docking **components**, airlocks, and living quarters that can house a crew of six. In order to provide a description of the International Space Station, it is necessary to **consider** the most important of these different **components**.

The **Integrated** Truss **Structure**

The length of a football field, the **Integrated** Truss **Structure**, sits atop and runs perpendicular to the Station's main living and **research** quarters. The most **visible feature** of the truss **structure** is its huge solar **panels**, which together supply enough power to light a small town. There are four pairs of **panels** on either side of the station, each 34 m long by 12 m wide, which the Solar Alpha Rotary Joint rotates in order to keep them pointed towards the sun. Other important **components** of the truss **structure** include a track which runs the length of the **structure** and upon which operates a 17.6-meter-long, 7-jointed, mobile robotic arm, a crew and **equipment** cart which can be used as a spacewalking platform, electrical cables, antennas, and the station's cooling and heating units. This truss **structure** is **integral** to the powering and **functioning** of the living and laboratory **sections** of the station.

The Zvezda and Zarya Service Modules

At the back of the main axis of the station is the **residential** quarters for three of the shuttle crew: the Zvezda Service Module. Weighing 19,000 tons,

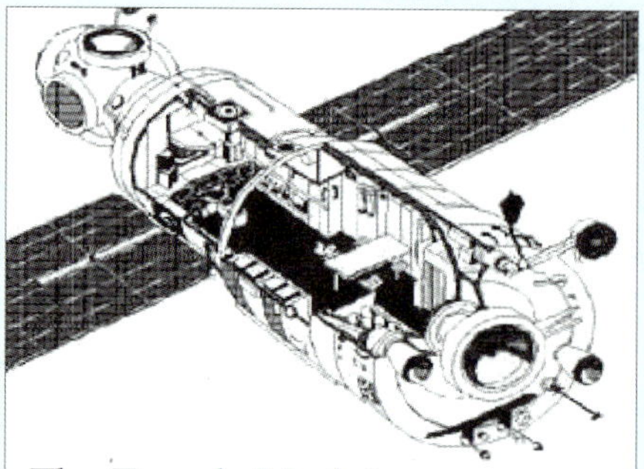
The Zvezda Module

its solar **panels** stretch out to almost 30 meters, while the main body is 19 meters long. Zvezda contains three pressurized chambers: a small, **spherical transfer** compartment and docking port at the front, the large living quarters in the middle, and another small **transfer** compartment and docking port at the back. Living accommodations include a toilet with hygiene **facilities**, a kitchen with a table, and sleeping **areas** for the crew. A stationary bicycle and treadmill have been provided for exercising. **Technical equipment** includes a life support system, **communication, data processing**, flight control and electrical **distribution**. With these **capabilities**, the Zvezda Service Module **demonstrates** Russian **expertise** in long-term space flight and is the **core** of her **contribution** to the International Space Station.

In front of the Zvezda Service Module is the Zarya module. It weighs 19,323 kilograms and is 12.6 meters long by 4.1 wide. Used **primarily** for its fuel tanks, which hold 5.4 tons of fuel and its storage **capability**, Zarya has large solar **panels** on either side. There are 3 docking modules: one each at the front and back and one on the side.

The Destiny Laboratory Module

Connected to the Zarya module by the Unity Module is the Destiny Laboratory Module. Destiny is the **primary** U.S. **research** laboratory. It holds 24 modular racks that can contain different **equipment** for experiments in a zero gravity **environment**, and which can be added or **removed** as necessary. The racks also contain water and oxygen recycling **equipment** that allows the International Space Station to regenerate these **crucial** supplies. Destiny is the control center for the station's robotic arm operations. It also has a fifty-centimeter-wide window, used to take high-**quality** video **images** of the earth. 8.53 meters long and 4.27 meters wide, the 14, 520 kg Destiny is a high-tech center of modern space experimentation, but it is not the only one on the station.

The Kibo and Columbus Experimental Modules

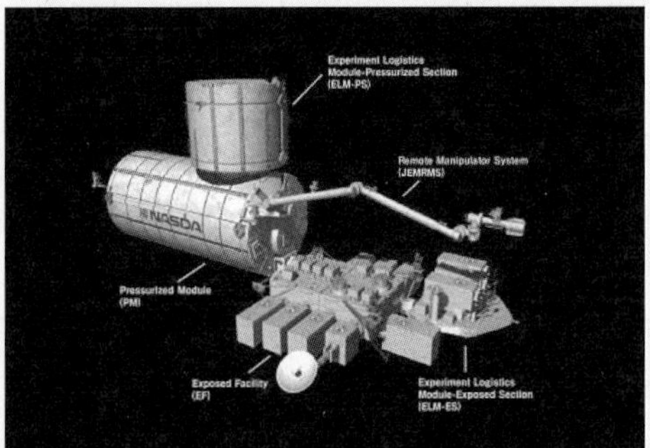

The Kibo Module

The Kibo Experimental Module, connected to the left side of the Harmony Module (containing living quarters for three), which connects to the forward end of Destiny, is the largest ISS module. It contains three sections: a pressurized module, about the size of a large bus (11.2 m × 4.4 m), an experimental pressurized module, which sits atop the main **section**, and an **exposed facility**, a platform 5.6 m wide, 5 m high and 4 m long. The pressurized module contains 23 experimental racks along with associated **communication** and life support **functions**, as well the controls for the Remote **Manipulator** System. This **consists** of two robotic arms that support operations outside Kibo. The **Exposed Facility** can contain up to ten experimental payloads that are **constantly exposed** space. Kibo is the center of Japanese **research** on the ISS.

Opposite Kibo, on the right side of Harmony, is the Columbus Module, 6.8 m long by 4.5 m wide. It can hold ten active International Standard Payload Racks inside its pressurized **environment**, eight in the walls, two in the ceiling, and four more outside in space. The inside racks host a variety of experiments that can be controlled by **researchers** on earth, inside their own laboratories, through the Columbus Control Center in Germany. The outside racks can be used to **investigate** anything from solar **phenomenon** to the ability of bacteria to **survive** on a meteorite. Columbus is the center of European Union activity on the ISS.

These main **components**, floating in space, stand testament to the international **partnership** which the International Space Station has brought about. Sixteen countries have **contributed** science, **technology** and astronauts on missions to the station, including the first five space tourists. **Conceivably**, this international collaboration in space could translate into greater international **cooperation** on Earth. Anyway, with additional **components**, upgrades and missions planned in the future, people will be permanently living upon the International Space Station for years to come.

Student B

Space Travel Sentence Dictation and Completion

1. Student B, stay here. Student A, go to page 35.
2. Your **partner** has the beginnings of the sentences below, and you have the ends.
3. Listen to your **partner** dictate the beginnings of the sentences and write them in where they belong.

---

a) ________________ is its huge solar **panels**, which together supply enough power to light a small town.

b) ______________________a kitchen with a table, and sleeping **areas** for the crew.

c) _________________400 kilometers above the earth at 27,700 kilometers per hour.

d) ________________ International Space Station to regenerate these crucial supplies.

e) ____ **research** laboratory.

Reading Strategy | Using a Dictionary

When you **encounter** a new word, sometimes you need to use a dictionary to discover its meaning. Unfortunately, there may be a number of meanings given. When this happens, look at the word in the **context** of the sentence, and look at the different meanings of the word in the dictionary. Is the word used as a noun, verb, adjective, or adverb? If you choose a good dictionary, there will also be example sentences, where the word is shown in **context**.

Consider this example

It can hold ten *active* International Standard Payload Racks inside its pressurized environment...

> *Active*[1] *Adj.* **1** *Someone who is active moves around a lot or does a lot of things. -Having an active youngster about the house can be quite wearing. ...a long and active life.* **2** *If you have an active mind or imagination, you are always thinking of new things. -...the tragedy of an active mind trapped by failing* ***physical*** *health.* **3** *If someone is active in an organization, cause or campaign, they do things for it rather than just giving it their support. -...a chance for fathers to play a more active* ***role*** *in childcare.* **4** *Active is used to* ***emphasize*** *that someone is taking action in order to* ***achieve*** *something, rather than just hoping for it or* ***achieving*** *it in an indirect way.-Companies need to take active steps to increase* ***exports****. ...active discouragement from teachers.* **5** *If you say that a person or animal is active in a particular place or time, you mean that they are performing their usual activities or performing a particular activity. -Guerilla groups are active in the province.* **6** *An active volcano has erupted recently or is expected to erupt quite soon. -...molten lava from an active volcano.*

---

1) Collins Cobuild Advanced Learner's English Dictionary, 5the **Edition**: Harper Collins, 2006.

Task 3-3

Which **definition** above most closely fits the meaning given in the sentence?

Reading Grammar : Pronoun Reference

One problem for readers of English is finding the original nouns to which pronouns refer. Here is an example.

In front of the Zvezda Service Module is the Zarya module. It weighs 19,323 kilograms and is 12.6 meters long by 4.1 wide.

"It" in the second sentence refers to "the Zarya module." This **illustrates** the **major** rule of pronoun reference: *a pronoun should refer to the closest* ***preceding*** *noun with which it agrees in* ***gender*** *and number.*

Task 3-4

Draw arrows from the pronouns to the nouns to which they refer in the following **selection**.

The length of a football field, the **Integrated** Truss **Structure**, sits atop and runs perpendicular to the Station's main living and **research** quarters. The most **visible feature** of the truss **structure** is its huge solar **panels**, which together supply enough power to light a small town. There are four pairs of **panels** on either side of the station, each 34 m long by 12 m wide, which the Solar Alpha Rotary Joint rotates in order to keep them pointed towards the sun. Other important **components** of the truss **structure** include a track which runs the length of the **structure** and upon which operates a 17.6-meter-long, 7-jointed mobile robotic arm, a crew and **equipment** cart which can be used as a spacewalking platform, electrical cables, antennas and the station's cooling and heating units.

Related Grammar: Agreement of Nouns, Pronouns and Verbs

Some of the first English lessons you probably learned were that English makes nouns plural by adding an "s," that pronouns must agree with these nouns, and that verbs must agree with both nouns and pronouns. **Research** shows, however, that this is one of the last things that Korean students learn to do well. Therefore, we will repeat it here.

Remember, some noun and verb plural forms are regular, and others are irregular. Here are some examples.

	Nouns		Verbs	
	Singular	Plural	Singular	Plural
Regular	girl	girls	likes	like
Irregular	child	children	has	have

Look at this example from the reading passage to see how *nouns*, <u>pronouns</u> and [verbs] agree with each other in a **text**.

At the *back* of the main *axis* of the *station* [is] the **residential** *quarters* for three of the shuttle *crew*: the Zvezda Service *Module*. Weighing 19,000 *tons*, <u>its</u> solar ***panels*** [stretch] out to almost 30 *meters*, while the main *body* [is] 19 *meters* long. <u>It</u> [contains] three pressurized *chambers*…

Task 3-5

The *nouns* and [verbs] are in base form, while the pronouns have been **removed** from this excerpt from the reading. Change them as necessary, and compare with the original **text**.

The Kibo Experimental *Module*, [connect] to the left *side* of the Harmony *module* ([contain] living *quarter* for three), ______ [connect] to the forward *end* of *Destiny*, [be] the largest ISS *module*. ______ [contain] three ***sections***: a pressurized *module*, about the [*size*] of a large *bus* (11.2 m × 4.4 m), an experimental pressurized *module*, ______ [sit] atop the main ***section***, and an **exposed** ***facility***, a *platform* 5.6 m wide, 5 m high and 4 m long. The pressurized *module* contain 23 experimental *rack* along with associated **communication** and life support ***function***, as well the *control* for the Remote **Manipulator** *System*. ______ consist of two robotic *arm* that support *operation* outside *Kibo*. The **Exposed *Facility*** can contain up to ten experimental *payload* ______ be **constantly** open to the *vacuum* of *space*. Kibo be the *center* of Japanese ***research*** on the *ISS*.

Comprehension Questions

Task 3-6

1. Look at the first **paragraph** of the reading passage and fill in the following **statistics**.

International Space Station	Size	Weight	Speed	Altitude	Crew	Modules

2. a) What is the main **function** of the **Integrated** Truss **Structure**?
   b) What other important **component**s does the **Integrated** Truss **Structure** **incorporate**?

3. List the **features** of the Zvezda Service Module.

4. a) How is the Destiny Module connected to the Zarya Module?
   b) What is the main **function** of Destiny?

5. How does the space station supply water and air for the astronauts on board?

6. Fill in the following **chart** to **display** the **similarities** and differences between the Kibo and Columbus modules.

	Kibo	Columbus
Differences		
Similarities		

7. Which is the most advanced laboratory: Destiny, Kibo or Columbus? Support your answer.

Reaction Questions

Task 3-7

Discuss the following questions with a **partner**.

1. Would you like to be an astronaut? Why or why not?
2. What is your opinion of space exploration? Is it a waste of **resources** and time, or an essential part of the modern world? Why?
3. Do you believe in aliens or UFOs?
4. Write one more question that you would like to ask your **partner** about the **topic**.

   ▶ ____

5. Write 100 to 150 words on one of the **topics** above. Include five words from the **Academic** Word List, **highlighted** in bold.

Writing Strategy | Descriptive Paragraphs

Descriptive Details

In this unit, you will write a description. Descriptions are "word pictures" that tell how something looks, feels, smells, tastes, and/or sounds.

It is very important to express your exact meaning when describing something, and this is usually done through the vocabulary you **select**. In the next exercise, you will describe a picture to your **partner**. Be as exact as possible in your description. Rather than saying, "a circle in the picture," say "There is a circle with a diameter of 3 1/2 centimeters in the middle of the picture."

Task 3-8

Part A

1. **Partner** A, stay here. **Partner** B, go to page 48.
2. Describe this picture to your **partner** as best you can. Your **partner** will draw it.

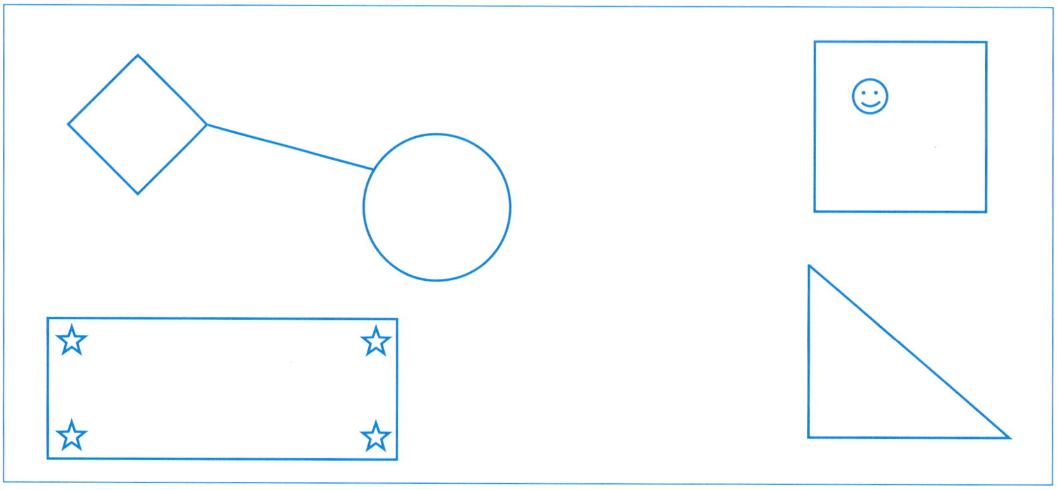

Part B

Now you will draw the picture your partner describes in the space below.

Specific Details

When you describe something, people should be able to close their eyes and "see," "hear," "smell," taste," or "touch" the thing you are describing. This is usually done either by a) comparing an object to something, b) giving the exact measurements, or c) using a better descriptive adjective.

Vague	Specific
The ISS is big	as big as two 747s
The ISS is big	500 tons and measuring 110 m x 95 m
The ISS is big	**enormous**

Task 3-9

Add **specific** details to these vague descriptions. Compare the thing being described to something else, give its exact measurement, and try a better descriptive adjective.

1. My brother is big.

a) ____________________

b) ____________________

c) ____________________

2. My boss has a nice house.

a) ____________________

b) ____________________

c) ____________________

3. The food tastes bad.

a) ____________________

b) ____________________

c) ____________________

4. The bus was crowded.

a) ______________________________

b) ______________________________

c) ______________________________

5. He was a good student.

a) ______________________________

b) ______________________________

c) ______________________________

Part A

1. Partner B, stay here. Partner A, go to page 46.
2. Draw the picture your partner describes in the space below.

Part B

Now describe this picture to your partner. Your partner will draw it.

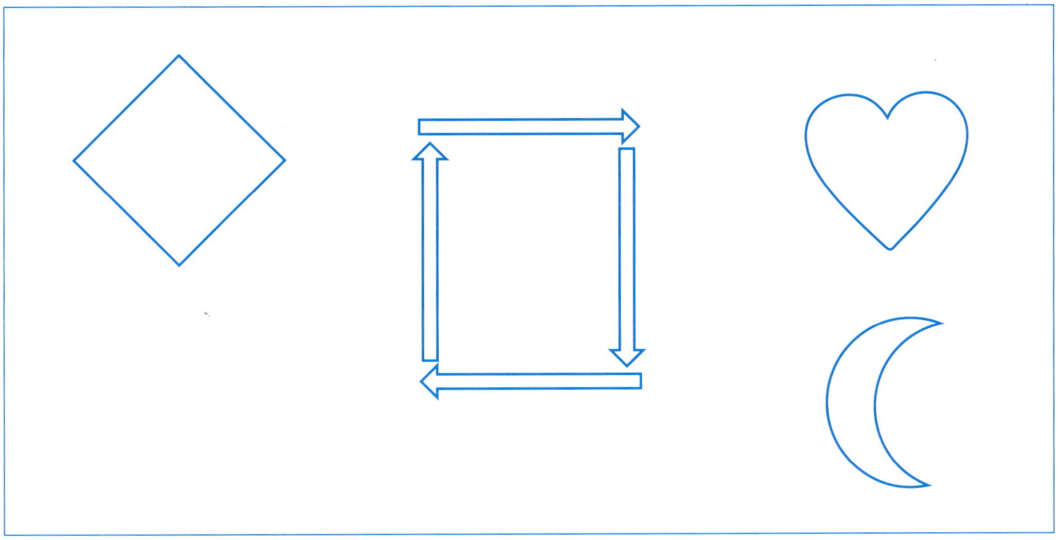

Organization in Descriptive Writing

Descriptive writing can be organized by *space*. When you organize your descriptive **paragraph** using *space order*, you describe where each person, place, or thing is **located** in relation to others.

The main idea is to move in a **logical** manner so that one thing follows another, rather than at **random** around an **area**. Also, finish describing one thing completely before you move on to the next. In space order, you might describe something from top to bottom, far to near, outside to inside, front to back, or right to left.

Task 3-10

1. Read the **paragraph** below, **analyze** the organization and fill in the outline that follows the **paragraph**.
2. Decide which space order it uses.

The Modern Spacesuit

NASA's new spacesuit is an **innovative** combination of **components designed** to offer an astronaut **maximum** mobility, comfort and protection while performing **tasks exposed** to the vacuum of space. The spacesuit's helmet is made of clear, impact-resistant, polycarbonate plastic, and the inside is treated with an anti-fog **chemical**. Over the helmet is fitted the extravehicular visor **assembly**, which has a metallic, gold-covered visor to filter sunlight, four head lamps, and a camera. Connected to the helmet with a quick-connect ring, the hard upper torso is a fiberglass shell in the shape of a vest which protects an astronaut's body. It supports the life-support backpack, the arms, and the lower torso of the suit. The backpack contains oxygen tanks, carbon dioxide scrubbers, cooling water, radio, electrical power, and ventilating fans. It allows the astronaut to **adjust** the temperature, pressure and air flow. Arms are made of fabric, but contain hard shoulder, upper arm and elbow joints so that the astronaut has **maximum flexibility** and protection. Gloves fit into the arms, have wrist bearings for **flexibility**, and have rubberized fingertips to help astronauts **manipulate** objects. The lower torso **assembly**, also made of **flexible** fabric, includes pants with knee and ankle joints and boots. **Finally**, inside all this, the astronaut wears a liquid cooling and ventilation garment, a set of "long underwear" containing thin plastic tubes through which cool water and gas flow. Taken together, this spacesuit **ensures** an astronaut's safety and comfort for up to seven hours outside the **confines** of a space ship.

Title

Topic Sentence

A: *The helmet – **clear** plastic, with a gold-covered visor over it* ____________

B: ____

C: ____

D: ____

E: ____

F: ____

G: ____

Concluding Sentence

Space Order: ____

Sentence Building: **Prepositional** Phrases

A prepositional phrase is a group of words that begins with a preposition, and includes at least a noun after the preposition. Prepositional phrases generally **function** in a sentence either as nominals, adjectives, or adverbs.

- Nominals replace nouns. In this case, the prepositional phrase is the subject of the sentence.

  (At the back of the main axis) is the **residential** quarters for three of the shuttle crew:

- Adjectives describe nouns. How many people are in the crew?

  living quarters that can house a crew (of six)

- Adverbs describe verbs. How does it hang?

  It hangs, (with its wings outstretched)

Task 3-11

Fill in the blanks in the following **paragraph** with the prepositional phrases in the box below.

around the Rover	during the day	from the front	Inside the body
like a human arm	of rocks and soil	of the Rover	on the surface of Mars
On top of the body	to a **suspension** system	with four tools	with NASA control

The Mars Explorer Rover

The Mars Explorer Rover is a mobile vehicle which acts as a robot geologist while ______________________. The Rover has six wheels. Each wheel is attached ____________ with an **individual** motor which prevents the Rover from flipping over. As well, the four front and back wheels also have individual steering motors, allowing the Rover to turn a full 360 degrees in place. The body ______________ is a strong, outer **layer** that protects the Rover's **computer**, electronics and batteries. ____________________, the Rover's **computer**, which is **equivalent** to a high-end laptop, **monitors** and controls the temperature, **communication** and **status** of the machine. _________________is a multi-array solar **panel**, which **generates** power _______________for two batteries inside the body. The Rover's "head and neck" is the Pancam Mast **Assembly**, 1.4 meters tall. The Pancam allows for a full 360 degree panoramic view of the **area** ______________. Other **mechanisms** sticking out from the top of the Rover include three antennae, used to **communicate** __________. **Finally**, a robotic arm extends _______________ of the Rover and holds and maneuvers the instruments that allow scientists to **analyze** the Martian **environment**. **Features** of the arm include a shoulder, elbow and wrist that allow it to maneuver ______________, and a "hand" at the end _________________. These tools can provide close-up **images** and **analyze** the composition ______________ that the Rover **encounters**. The Rover is a powerful **device** which has greatly **enhanced** our knowledge of the planet Mars.

Task 3-12

Fill in the blanks in the sentences below, and then check them in the article at the beginning of the chapter.

1. It hangs, _____ its wings outstretched, looking _____ a high-tech **version** _____ an old-fashioned flying machine.
2. This machine does not fly _____ the air; it orbits 400 kilometers _____ the earth _____ 27,700 kilometers per hour.
3. It is the same size _____ two 747s.

4. The length _____ a football field, the **Integrated** Truss **Structure**, sits _____ and runs perpendicular _____ the Station's main living and **research** quarters.

5. _____ the _____ _____ the main axis _____ the station is the **residential** quarters _____ three _____ the shuttle crew: the Zvezda Service Module.

Task 3-13

Fill in the blanks in the paragraph below with the correct prepositions from the box..

at	a	for	for	from	from	of	of	of	off
on	to	to	top	under	underneath		underneath		

Man _____ the Moon

The Saturn 5 rocket carried the Apollo astronauts _____ the moon and was the largest and most powerful rocket that has ever been made. _____ the _____ of the rocket was the Apollo Command Module. The Apollo Command Module orbited the moon waiting _____ the Lunar Module and re-entered the earth's atmosphere, bringing the astronauts home. The Lunar Module was _____ the Command Module. The Lunar Module **consisted** _____ two **sections**: the descent stage, which landed _____ the moon, and the ascent stage, which separated _____ the descent stage and blasted _____ _____ the moon. The third stage rocket _____ the Saturn 5 used liquid oxygen and hydrogen _____ fuel and was positioned _____ the Command Module. _____ the third stage was the second stage, which used the same fuel. The first stage, burning liquid oxygen and kerosene, was _____ the bottom _____ the rocket. The Saturn 5 was 110.6 meters tall, 10.1 meters wide, and weighed 3,038,500 kilograms.

Academic Vocabulary Development

Task 1-2 **Nouns**

You must put the word that follows the sentence into its correct noun form and use it to fill in the blank in the sentence. Check these sentences with the original sentences from the **text** to see how different word forms are used.

1. At the back of the main axis of the station is the ________ for three of the shuttle crew: **(residential)** (37)
2. The small, pressurized **transfer** and docking compartment at the front of Zvezda is shaped like a ________ . **(spherical)** (38)
3. The Zvezda Service Module is an excellent ________ of Russian **expertise** in long-term space flight. **(demonstrates)** (38)
4. The addition or ________ of modular racks from the Destiny Laboratory Module can be **conducted** as necessary. **(removed)** (38)
5. The **Exposed Facility** can contain up to 10 experimental payloads that **maintain constant** ________ to the vacuum of space. **(exposed)** (39)
6. The outside racks can be used for the ________ of anything from solar **phenomenon** to the ________ of bacteria on a meteorite. (**investigate, survive**) (39)
7. The ________ of science, **technology** and astronauts by sixteen countries to the station have led to international collaboration in space which could translate into greater international **cooperation** on Earth. (**contributed**) (40)
8. The combination of **components** offered an astronaut by NASA's extravehicular mobility unit is a huge ________ compared to what was **previously** available. (**innovative**) (50)
9. It allows the astronaut to do a temperature ________ . (**adjust**) (50)

Academic Writing Assignment: Descriptive Paragraph

Write a paragraph that describes one of the following. Use at least five words from the **Academic** Word List that have appeared in the book so far. Type the words in bold so that your teacher can easily identify them.

1. Do some **research** and describe a space-based piece of machinery.
2. Describe a machine in your home, such as a computer or car.
3. Describe your room, a crowded bus or a crowded subway.
4. Describe something with the approval of your teacher.

The Writing Process

1. Planning: Free Writing There are various ways of getting ideas, and free writing is among the most useful. The idea is very simple. Just write whatever comes into your mind about the **topic** for a limited **period** of time. Don't stop to think about grammar, **relevance**, or vocabulary. You may write **individual** words, but not sentences, in Korean, if that helps you. You will **edit** for grammar, **relevance** and vocabulary later.

For this exercise, you will free write about the **topic** you have chosen for ten minutes. DON'T STOP. Just write.

2. After you have finished, **edit** your original piece of free writing. Decide which ideas you want to include in your **paragraph** and which you want to omit. Combine ideas that belong together. Cross out words that repeat the same ideas. Cross out ideas that are not directly related to the main idea. Add details to better describe what you are describing.

3. Outline Now make a **paragraph** outline for your **paragraph**. Use space order to make your outline flow **logically**. Be sure the most important **structures** are included. Make sure you fully describe one **item** before you move on to the next. Are you describing something well enough that a person who has never seen it

before would be able to "see" it in their mind? Be sure to describe in detail shape, size and color. Write a **topic** sentence that gives a broad description of the object being described. Write a **concluding** sentence that leaves the reader with a strong impression. See page 51 for an example.

4. First Draft Now you should **refine** your outline into a first **draft** for your **paragraph**. Write out the ideas from your outline into full sentences in the body of your **paragraph**. Be sure all the sentences in the body are **relevant** to and support the **topic** sentence. Avoid repetition. Write a title that will capture the reader's attention.

5. Edit Check the **paragraph** against the **paragraph** checklist on the next page and make corrections.

6. Final Draft Type an 8 – 12 sentence **paragraph** and hand it in to the teacher.

Descriptive Paragraph Checklist

Form

- Is the paragraph typed in 12-point type and double-spaced?
- Are there 8 to 12 sentences?
- Is the first line of the paragraph indented?
- Does one sentence directly follow the next (don't write new sentences on new lines)?

Organization

- Does the **topic** sentence give a broad description of the object being described?
- Are all the sentences **relevant**?
- Is there any redundancy?
- Does the **paragraph** have a **logical** order?
- Is there an effective **concluding** sentence?

Content

- Does the writer engage the reader's interest in the title and **topic** sentence?
- Is the paragraph direct and clear?
- Does the **paragraph** paint a successful "mind picture?"
- Does the **paragraph** use a variety of sentence **structures**?
- Are there 5 words from the **Academic** Word List in bold?

Grammar and Mechanics

- Does the writer avoid mistakes of spelling, capitalization and punctuation?
- Are there any mistakes of singular or plural?
- Does the writer avoid sentence fragments?
- Are adjectives used correctly?
- Does the writer use correct verb **tenses**?
- Are **coordinating** conjunctions used correctly?
- Do the nouns, pronouns and verbs agree with each other?
- Are prepositional phrases used correctly?

Chapter

04 Korean Geography

Student A

Korean Geography Quiz

1. Student A, stay here. Student B, go to page 66.
2. Read the questions to your **partner**. The answers are underlined, but don't tell your **partner**. Is she correct or incorrect?
3. Listen to your **partner**'s questions. Do you know the answers?

---

1. South and North Korea together have a total land **area** of:
   a. 200,000 square. kilometers. b. 210,000 sq.km. c. 240, 000 sq.km.
2. How high is Mt. Halla?
   a. 1,950 meters b. 1,960m c. 1,970 m
3. How long is the Han River?
   a. 464 kilometers b. 514 km c. 564 km
4. What is the average **annual** precipitation in Seoul?
   a. 1144 millimeters b. 1244 millimeters c. 1344 millimeters
5. What is the average temperature in Seoul in January?
   a. -3º C b. 0º C c. +3º C

Focus Question

Task 4-1

Describe the weather, geography and most common plants and animals of the Korean peninsula to a **partner**.

Task 4-2 Vocabulary

Match the words on the left with their **definitions** on the right.

1. _____ a deciduous tree
2. _____ elevation
3. _____ an evergreen
4. _____ a mammal
5. _____ a monsoon
6. _____ temperate climate
7. _____ tundra
8. _____ a typhoon

a) a tree with long, pointed leaves that stay on all year

b) a tree with broad leaves that fall off in autumn

c) a rainy season

d) a big storm with wind and rain

e) four seasons with a relatively mild winter

f) a warm-blooded animal that gives birth to live young and feeds them on milk from the mother

g) the height of a particular **area** of the earth

h) arctic vegetation characterized by grasses and flowers with no trees

Reading Strategy | Scanning for Information

Task 4-3 There is one extra **paragraph** that does not belong in the following composition. Quickly scan the **text**, find the extra **paragraph**, and cross it out from the reading passage.

Ecoregions of Korea

In a 2001 study, the World Wildlife **Fund defined** an ecoregion as a "large unit of land or water containing a geographically **distinct assemblage** of species, natural **communities**, and **environmental** conditions." In this **project**, the WWF determined that the Korean Peninsula has four **distinct** ecoregions. These four Korean ecoregions are, from south to north: the Southern Korea Evergreen Forests, the Central Korean Deciduous Forests, the Manchurian Mixed Forests and the White Head Mountains Mixed Forests.

Despite their **distinctiveness**, the boundaries of the ecoregions blend into each other, so that there are **transition** zones and some **similarities** between them. In the Korean **context**, some important **features** across all ecoregions are the low mountains that cover 70% of the peninsula and a climate (the general weather conditions in an **area** over a **period** of time) that slowly **transitions** to cooler and drier from south to north. These **regions** are partly **unique** to Korean, but also share characteristics with ecoregions in neighboring and far away countries.

Southern Korean Evergreen Forests

As part of the East Asian Monsoonal **Region**, this **area** is mostly cool and dry in the winter and hot and sticky in summer, with two-thirds of the almost 1,500 mm of **annual** precipitation, or forms of water that fall from the sky, coming from June to September. On Cheju Island, the average temperature is 3ºC in January and 25ºC in July, so that its winters are warmer than in other **areas** of Korea. There are fewer typhoons than in neighboring countries such as Japan and Taiwan.

This relatively wet and warm climate influences vegetation. At the southern tip of the Korean Peninsula, including Cheju and Ullong Islands, there are warm-temperate to subtropical evergreen broadleaf forests. As in the

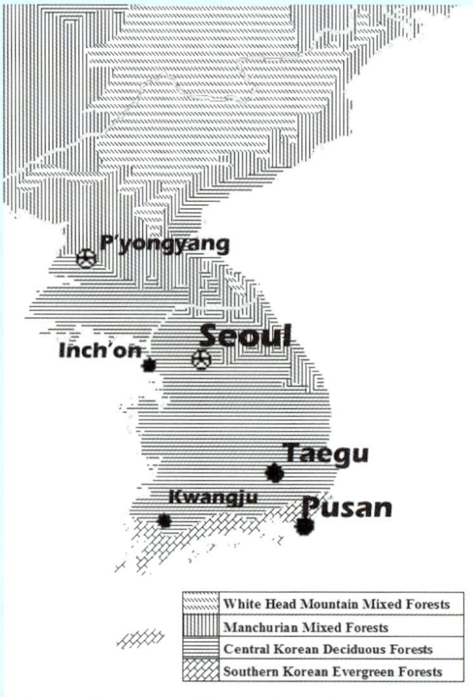

rest of the peninsula, the southern coast and islands are mountainous; **hence** flora (plant life in a **region**) **varies** greatly according to elevation, but generally it is typical of the warm-temperate zone that stretches from southern Japan to the foothills of the Himalayas. Characteristic tree species include the Asian Hornbeam, the laurel, different types of oak, tea bushes, bamboo and the Camphor tree. Human activity has greatly reduced the **range** of these forests, though good examples remain in Ulsan, Hampyeong and Naejang-san.

This is **potentially** the most bio-**diverse area** of Korea. Most of the 379 bird species recorded in South Korea pass through this **region** due to its mild winter climate. Rare bird species include the White-Bellied Black Woodpecker, the Fairy Pitta and the Ring-Necked Pheasant. Roe Deer and weasels live on Cheju Island today, but wild boar and wild cats are now extinct on the island. Although reforestation has been successful in mountainous **areas**, most of the lowlands have been **converted** to agriculture, so that species **range** and **diversity** has been limited.

Central Korean Deciduous Forests

Found north of the Arctic Circle in Russia, Canada and Norway, the Arctic Desert ecoregion is one of the most northern and **isolated** landscapes on Earth. The ecoregion is made of several island groups that are surrounded by ice most of the year. Temperatures are very cold, from an average of -30ºC in February to -1ºC in July. The sparse vegetation **consists** of mosses, lichens and low grasses.

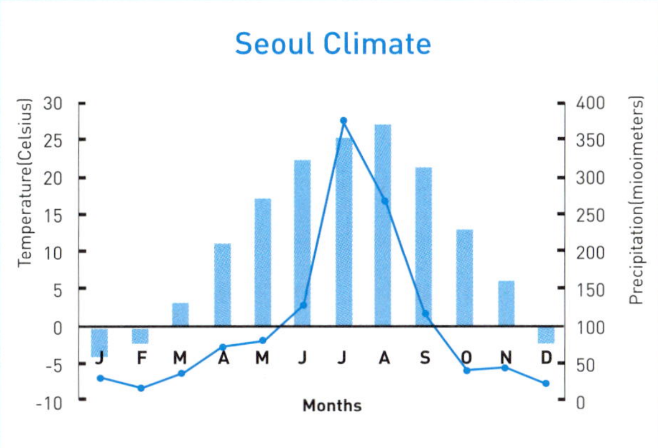

Again, the Central Korean Deciduous Forests ecoregion is similar to all of Korea in that it is part of the East Asian monsoonal **region**, Summer temperatures resemble those further south, while winter temperatures average -4ºC in January. Detailed precipitation and temperature patterns can be seen on the left.

There is **sufficient** precipitation and temperature to support a deciduous forest that **varies** from south to north, while evergreens **occur** in the cold mountains. Common tree species in the **region** include pine, maple, oak, fir, birch, ash, walnut, willow, elm, snowbell, hornbeam and bamboo, although different species of the same tree may be more plentiful from north to south; for example, the most common oak species in the southern part of the **region** is *Quercus acutissima*, while in the northern parts, *Quercus mongolica* **dominates**. This vegetation is the most **widespread** and characteristic of Korea.

The fauna, or animal species **found** in an **area**, of this ecoregion resembles that **found** in **adjacent regions** of Japan and China. Large predators such as wolves, tigers, leopards and bears were once common, but are now either extinct or very rare, while smaller predators such as weasels, badgers and martins still exist in remote mountain **areas**. Mammals such as deer and wild boar are still relatively plentiful. Endangered birds include the Crested Shelduck, Red-Crowned Cranes, White–Naped Cranes, and the White-Bellied

Black Woodpecker. Because of its **status** as a no-go zone, the Demilitarized Zone between North and South Korea has become a critical habitat for some of these species.

Manchurian Mixed Forests

The climate is monsoonal in summer, with a longer, colder winter because of continental influences from the Asian interior. Average January temperatures are between -10ºC and -15ºC and from 22ºC to 24ºC in August. Precipitation averages about 1,000 mm **annually**. There is typically one typhoon a summer.

Corresponding to the cooler temperatures, there are more evergreens here than in the south, and more towards the north and at higher elevations. These include the Korean Pine, the Siberian Spruce, and fir. Deciduous species include oaks, ash, birch, Manchurian Elm, maple, and Manchurian Walnut.

While tigers, sables and leopards still exist in the Chinese and Russian parts of the Manchurian Mixed Forests ecoregion; they are probably extinct in the Korean section. As in Central Korean deciduous forests, deer, wild boar and black bear, along with smaller mammalian species, are present in more remote **areas**.

White Head Mountain Mixed Forests

This **area**, which surrounds and includes White Head Mountain, is the highest, most northerly, and most remote part of the Korean peninsula. Because of the great **range** in elevation, bioclimatic zones **vary** from temperate in the valleys to alpine (high mountain) tundra at high elevations. The long, cold winters have an average January temperature of between -10ºC and -20ºC, while the monsoon brings summer rain and average August temperatures of between 18 and 20ºC. Lower elevations receive 500 to 1000 mm of precipitation **annually**, while higher elevations may receive more.

Lower zones have mixed forest with deciduous species resembling those in the Manchurian Mixed Forests Zone such as Mongolian oak, ash, and dwarf birch. As the elevation increases, the colder temperatures act as a **constraint** upon species **diversity**. From 500 to 1,100 meters elevation, evergreens such as Korean Pine, fir, red pine and Japanese Yew **dominate**. At 1,100 to 1,500 m., spruce, fir and larch prevail. Between 1,500 and 1,900 m, Jezo Spruce and the Eastern Siberian Fir are the **dominant** tree species. Higher than that are only alpine bushes, shrubs and grasses.

Because of its **isolated** nature, this is the only **region** of Korea where there still may be tigers, leopards and wolves, as well as the large mammalian species **found** further south. Rare bird species include the Black Grouse, Hazel Grouse, Black Stork, Mandarin Duck, Oriental Stork and Scaly-sided Merganser.

The four Korean ecoregions **compose** four **distinct areas**, with **discrete** climates, flora and fauna. However, they also share common characteristics such as the influence of continental and monsoonal climates, mountain and valley landscapes, and **assemblages** of plants and animals that change gradually rather than abruptly. The World Wildlife **Fund** has, in the same way, divided the whole world into 687 ecoregions, of which the four in Korea are but a small part. If you want to know more, go to their website, www.worldwildlife.org.

Student B

Korean Geography Quiz

1. Student B, stay here. Student A, go to page 59.
2. Listen to your **partner**'s questions. Do you know the answer?
3. Ask your **partner** these questions. The answers are underlined, but don't tell your **partner**. Is he correct or incorrect?

---

1. The population of Seoul is about:

   a. 8.4 million b. 9.4 million c. <u>10.4 million</u>

2. The average **annual** precipitation of Pyongyang is:

   a. 725 millimeters b. 825 millimeters c. <u>925 millimeters</u>

3. The average low temperature in January in Pyongyang is:

   a. <u>-10º C</u> b. -5º C c. 0º C

4. How tall is Baekdu mountain?

   a. 2644 meters b. <u>2744 meters</u> c. 2844 meters

5. The Nakdong River is Korea's longest river. How long is it?

   a. <u>526 kilometers</u> b. 576 kilometers c. 626 kilometers

Reading Strategy | Classification

Task 4-4 In a classification essay, **similar** things are **categorized** according to several **criteria**. **Criteria** are standards that we can use to compare things to each other. For example, in a comparison of two cities, one might judge them according to population, climate and tourist attractions. In this essay, three **criteria** were used to classify the ecoregions. What were they?

	Criterion 1	Criterion 2	Criterion 3
Southern Korean Evergreen Forest			
Central Korean Deciduous Forest			
Manchurian Mixed Forest			
Whitehead Mountain Mixed Forest			

Reading Strategy — Definition

Task 4-5 **Technical** vocabulary will often be **defined** in a **text** as it is presented. In the reading passage above, six words were **defined**. Write the words and their **definitions**.

Comprehension Questions

Task 4-6

1. Where are there the fewest typhoons: Japan, Taiwan, or Korea?
2. What type of forest **dominates** in the Southern Korean Evergreen Forest?
3. Which species have become extinct on Cheju Island?
4. What has limited species **range** and bio-**diversity** in the Southern Korean Evergreen Forest?
5. a) In which month does Seoul get the most precipitation?
   b) When does Seoul get the least precipitation?
   c) Which month is the coldest in Seoul?
   d) Which is the warmest?
6. How does flora and fauna **vary** between lowland and mountain in the Central Korean Deciduous Forests ecoregions?
7. Which vegetation is most characteristic of the Korean peninsula?
8. Fill in the **chart** on the next page.

	Manchurian Mixed Forests		Central Korean Deciduous Forests
	Differences	**Similarities**	Differences
Climate			
Flora			
Fauna			

9. What kind of vegetation **dominates** at the highest elevations of the White Head Mountain Mixed Forests ecoregion?

10. a) What species may be present in the White Head Mountain Mixed Forests ecoregion that may not exist elsewhere in Korea?
    b) Why are these species present here?

11. How can you find more information?

Reaction Questions

Task 4-7

Discuss the following questions with a **partner**.

1. Which Korean city, province, or ecoregion would you most like to live in? Why?
2. Choose an a) animal, b) bird, c) tree, or d) flower that best represents Korea. Why do you say that?
3. Which countries in the world do you think are most like Korea? Why? Which ones are most different from Korea? Why?

4. Write one more question that you would like to ask your **partner** about the **topic**.

▶ ____

5. Choose one of the above and write 100 to 150 words explaining your answer. Include five words from the **Academic** Word List, **highlighted** in bold.

Writing Strategy | Comparison and Contrast Paragraphs

Comparison and **contrast** is a **method** of showing **similarities** and differences between subjects. You may do either or both in a **paragraph**. Are you trying to show that one side is better or only to show things are **similar** or different? If you want to show that one actor, one movie, one writer or one idea is better than another, your purpose is to persuade. You will **emphasize** the superiority of one side over the other in your **topic** sentence and in your support. If you want to explain something about a **topic** by showing each subject in relation to others, then your purpose is informative. For example, you might be comparing two historical figures, Napoleon and Alexander the Great. Both were **military** geniuses, so you may decide that it would be senseless to argue that one is superior to the other. Instead, you choose to **reveal** interesting information about both by comparing and **contrasting** them to each other.

Example Paragraph

Gapyong or Danyang: Make the Right Choice

Although Gapyong in Gyonggi-do is a fine weekend destination, Danyang, Choongcheon-do is a better place for a short getaway with your family. Gapyong is known for its hiking. Mount Myungji offers wide views, deep valleys, and **challenging** trails. **Similarly**, Danyong has Mount Seobaek, which is beautiful in all four seasons. Gapyong has less **varied** tourist attractions than Danyang. Gapyong has Nami Island, an overrated and rundown attraction on the Han River. Danyong, on the **contrary**, offers several spectacular caves, a large and **unique** Buddhist temple named Guin-sa and various other sights, including a spa, to keep a family entertained. However, the main reason that Danyong is a nicer place than Gapyong is the town itself. Gapyong is a regular sleepy town: nice, but nothing special. Danyong, on the other hand, is built on a ridge overlooking the South Han River, with a view of towering cliffs lined with waterfalls. Everywhere you look is a majestic view. While you have to go out of town to get great views in Gapyong, they are right outside your hotel window in Danyong. Why don't you go to both places to see if you agree?

Task 4-8

1. Fill in the following outline of the example **paragraph** above.

Organization by **Criteria**	
Title	
Topic Sentence	
Body • **Criterion A** – *hiking* Subject 1 – *Gapyong* Subject 2 – *Danyang* • **Criterion B** – Subject 1 – Subject 2 – • **Criterion C** – Subject 1 – Subject 2 -S	 evidence? –*Mt. Myungji* –*Mt. Seobaek* **evidence**? **evidence**?
Concluding Sentence	

2. Is the purpose of this paragraph to persuade or inform?

Organization in Comparison and **Contrast Paragraphs**

You will organize your **evidence** according to either **criteria** or subject. The example **paragraph** above organizes the information according to **criteria**. This shows the points in relation to the sides (subjects) one at a time. This is the more common pattern. Organization by subject, on the **contrary**, presents all one side and then all the other side.

Common types of **evidence** are examples, opinions, explanations, and **statistics**. Some **evidence** is better than others; however, the most important point that can be made about **evidence** is that it becomes more powerful the more **specific** and **relevant** it is. For example, in the **paragraph** above, the **author** compared hiking in Gapyong and Danyang, and gave as **evidence** two mountains that are commonly hiked. These are **specific** and **relevant** examples. Always provide **evidence** for any assertion that you make.

Task 4-9

Rearrange the information from the example **paragraph** and outline so that it fits in the outline for a subject-by-subject pattern.

Organization by Subject	
Title	
Topic Sentence	
Body	
• Subject 1 –*Gapyong*	
Criterion A -*hiking*	**evidence** – *Mt. Myungji*
Criterion B	**evidence?**
Criterion C	**evidence?**
• Subject 2	
Criterion A	**evidence?**
Criterion B	**evidence?**
Criterion C	**evidence?**
Concluding Sentence	

Language Patterns in Comparison and **Contrast Paragraphs**

Task 4-10

Fill in the patterns below with information from the example **paragraph**

•Patterns to show concession

Even though *Gapyong* ____________________, *Danyang* ____________________.

Although ____.

While ____.

Gapyong __________________; **nevertheless**, *Danyang*____________________.

__________________________; **nonetheless**, _________________________.

•Patterns to show similarities

Gapyong __________________; **similarly**, *Danyang* ____________________.

__________________________; **likewise**,____________________________.

__________________________; in the same way,________________________.

Both Gapyong and Danyang ____.

Similar to ____.

•Patterns to show differences

Gapyong __________________; in **contrast**, *Danyang*____________________.

__________________________; on the other hand,________________________.

__________________________; however, _____________________________.

__________________________; on the **contrary**, ________________________.

Different from *Gapyong, Danyang* ______________________________________.

Unlike ____.

Task 4-11

1. Fill in the blanks to make **appropriate** language patterns. There may be more than one correct answer.

Hiking in Seoul

_______ Nam Mountain and Pukhan Mountain in Seoul are great hiking courses; _______, Pukhan is for the more hard-**core element**. There are several ways up Nam Mountain, including steps or a cable car. If you decide to walk, it is an easy climb for someone in good shape. Once you are at the top, Nam Mountain is downtown, so it offers great views of the Han River and central Seoul. The top of the mountain is developed, with the iconic Seoul Tower, and various other parks, gardens and sights at the bottom, along the slopes or at the top. Pukhan Mountain, _________ , takes some real effort. At 854 meters, it is the tallest mountain in the Seoul **area**. __________ Nam Mountain, Pukhan Mountain is easily **accessible** by bus or subway. Because it is **located** in northern Seoul, Pukhan Mountain has larger views of northern Seoul than Nam Mountain, and the various other mountains and **areas** in the surrounding northern Kyunggi-do **area**. On **clear** days, you can see the sea. _________ the base of Pukhan offers many restaurants and rest areas, the upper slopes are a rocky, steep and relatively pristine **environment** where wild animals such as wild boars and hawks still live. If you are lucky, you might see one. If you are going for a day hike, Nam Mountain and Pukhan Mountain are both enjoyable; _________ , you need to be **aware** of the differences.

2. Is the purpose of the paragraph to persuade or inform?

Sentence Grammar: Comparatives with Nouns

Everybody has studied how to make comparative adjectives:

The boy is shorter than the man.

Shiela is more **intelligent** than Janie.

We can, however, also make comparatives using nouns. They often look like this:

• A+verb + more/less/fewer+noun or noun phrase+than B.

Danyong has more tourist attractions than Gapyong.

• A+verb+comparative adjective+noun or noun phrase+than B.

Pukhan Mountain offers larger views of northern Seoul than Nam Mountain

Task 4-12

Write sentences using comparatives. Check the text above for the answers.

1. There/few/typhoon/ in neighboring countries such as Japan and Taiwan.

▶ ______________________________

2. The climate is monsoonal in summer, with/long/cold/winter.

▶ ______________________________

3. Corresponding to/ cool/temperature, there/evergreen here/in the south.

▶ ______________________________

Task 4-13

Write sentences using the following cues. If necessary, change the adjectives to their comparative forms and change the nouns to their plural forms.

Korea's East and West Coasts

1. East Coast/(+)mountain/West Coast

   ⊙ ______________________________

2. East Coast/(-)large river flowing into it/West Coast

   ⊙ ______________________________

3. East Coast/(-)island/West Coast

   ⊙ ______________________________

4. East Coast/(-)fertile agricultural **region**/West Coast

   ⊙ ______________________________

5. East Coast/(+)beautiful beach/West Coast

   ⊙ ______________________________

6. East Coast/(+)deep beach/West Coast

   ⊙ ______________________________

7. East Coast/(+)clean/cold water/West Coast

   ⊙ ______________________________

8. East Coast/(+)cool weather/West Coast

   ⊙ ______________________________

9. East Coast/(-)mud flat/West Coast

   ⊙ ______________________________

10. East Coast/(-)people/West Coast

    ⊙ ______________________________

Academic Vocabulary Development

Task 4-14 Adverbs

You must put the word that follows the sentence into its correct adverbial form and use it to fill in the blank in the sentence. Check these sentences with the original sentences from the **text** to see how different word forms are used.

1. The **benefits** are _________ limitless. (**potential**) (9)
2. Look at the word ____________ in the sentence. (**context**) (41)
3. The main idea is to move ____________ so that one thing follows another, rather than __________ around an **area**. (**logical, random**) (49)
4. The arms are made of fabric, but contain hard shoulder, upper arm, and elbow joints to be ____________ **flexible**. (**maximum**) (50)
5. The four front and back wheels are steered ___________ (**individual**) (53)
6. These **regions** are partly ____________ Korean, but also share characteristics with ecoregions in neighboring and far away countries. (**unique**) (61)
7. How much precipitation is there ____________ in Seoul? (**annual**) (61)
8. It precipitates _________ to support a deciduous forest.(**sufficient**) (63)
9. Danyong, ____________, offers several spectacular caves. (**contrary**) (69)

Academic Writing Assignment: Compare and Contrast Paragraph

Write a **paragraph** about one of the following topics. Use at least five words from the **Academic** Word List that have appeared in the book so far.

1. Compare and **contrast** two cities, either in Korea or elsewhere.
2. Compare and **contrast** two rivers.
3. Compare and **contrast** two mountains.
4. Compare and **contrast** two other things, with the approval of your teacher.

The Writing Process

1. Planning:

You may find it useful to make an organizer like this. Use it to list as many points of comparison and **contrast** as you can. Set a time limit, say, 10 minutes.

Item 1		Item 2
Differences	**Similarities**	Differences

Now **select** the three best points of **contrast** and comparison from your list for a deep and meaningful **paragraph**. In other words, if you are comparing two oceans, don't waste time by noting that both are blue. Provide **specific** and **relevant evidence** for your points of **contrast** and comparison.

2. Outline Make an outline. Write a **topic** sentence, and choose a criteria or subject-by-subject **method** as on pages 70 and 71. Make sure that your three points are **relevant** to your **topic** sentence. Write a **concluding** sentence and a title.

3. First Draft Write a first **draft**.

4. Editing Check your first **draft** against the **paragraph** checklist below.

5. Final Draft Type a **final draft** to hand into your teacher.

Checklist For Comparison and **Contrast Paragraph**

Form
- Does the **paragraph** use correct **paragraph** form?

Organization
- Is there a **topic** sentence with a **topic** and a controlling idea?
- Are all the sentences **relevant**?
- Is there any redundancy?
- Does the **paragraph** follow a point-by-point or subject-by-subject order?
- Is there an effective **concluding** sentence?

Content
- Does the paragraph engage the reader's interest in the title and **topic** sentence?
- Is the **paragraph** direct and **clear**?
- Does the **paragraph** use a variety of sentence **structures** to make the **paragraph** more interesting?
- Are the three points of comparison deep and meaningful?
- Is there **relevant evidence** to support the comparisons?
- Are there five words from the Academic Word List in bold?

Grammar and Mechanics
- Does the writer avoid mistakes of spelling, capitalization and punctuation?
- Are there any mistakes of singular or plural?
- Does the writer avoid sentence fragments?
- Does the writer use correct verb **tenses**?
- Are **coordinating** conjunctions used correctly?
- Do the nouns, pronouns and verbs agree with each other?
- Are prepositional phrases used correctly?
- Does the writer use comparison and **contrast structures** correctly?
- Are noun, verb, adjective and adverb forms used correctly?

05 Scientific Controversies

Student A

Scientific Controversies Information Gap

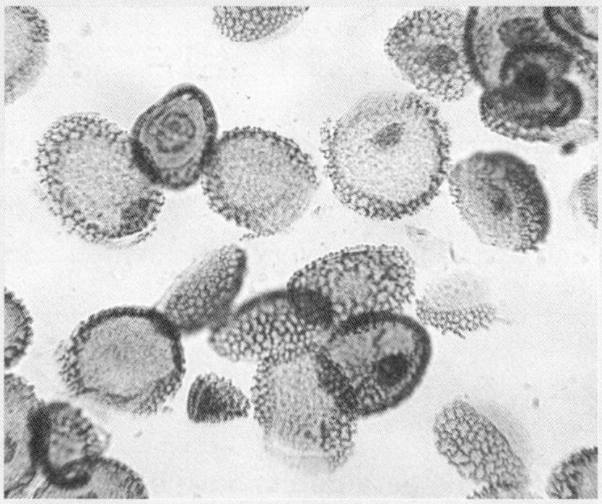

1. Student A, stay here. Student B, go to page 84.
2. The words and phrases are from the article below. Read them to your **partner** so that she can match them with the **definitions** she has.
3. Match your **definitions** with the words your **partner** provides.

organic	primitive	atmosphere	biosphere	amino acid

a) __________ to bring about a **chemical reaction**

b) __________ a substance that has a regular, repeating arrangement of atoms and often of **external** plane surfaces

c) __________ a tiny, living being, too small to be seen with the **unaided** eye

d) __________ the smallest particle of matter that is **chemically** the same as the whole mass of which it is a part

e) __________ able to reproduce by itself

Focus Question

Task 5-1

Tell your **partner** what you know about the origin of life on Earth.

Reading Strategy | Topic Sentences

Topic Sentences are not always the first sentence of a **paragraph**. Writers can move these around for different effects. However, they are recognizable because they both contain the main idea of the **paragraph** and are related to every other sentence in it.

Task 5-2

In the article below, the **topic** sentences of all the **paragraphs** have been **removed**. **Insert** the **topic** sentences back into their proper places in the article.

a) First proposed in 1924, Aleksandr Oparin's **chemical** soup **theory** stated that a soup of organic molecules was **created** in Earth's primitive, oxygen-free atmosphere through the action of sunlight and lightning.

b) In his deep, hot biosphere **theory** of 1992, Gold proposed that life developed several kilometers under the surface of the Earth.

c) life could have originated through **chemical reactions** using **complex** clay molecules as a sort of scaffold.

d) The aforementioned Francis Crick was a supporter of the idea that life might have originally formed either in space or on Mars, and been **transported here**.

e) There are several **assumptions** upon which most of the warring **researchers** agree.

How Did We Get Here?

"The origin of life appears...to be almost a miracle," so **commented** Francis Crick, the co-discoverer of the DNA molecule. This statement **illustrates** the fact that there is very little agreement among scientists to one of the central questions of existence: abiogenesis, or the origin of life on Earth. Every **culture** ever known has had some sort of **creation** myth: humans seem to have a deep need to understand where we come from. A conclusive answer, however, has eluded modern science. What modern science offers are several models that compete with each other for **validity**. Among them are the **chemical** soup **hypothesis**, clay **theory**, the deep, hot biosphere model and the primitive extraterrestrial life **theory**.

1)____

____

First, they agree that life originated from lifelessness. Somehow, organic, self-replicating organisms came to be where there had **previously** been none. Also, most scientists now concur that life began on Earth between 4.4 and 3.5 billion years ago. Since the Earth itself is thought to be about 5.5 billion years old and was unsuitable for life for the first 500 to 800 million years, life appeared relatively early in the history of the planet. Now that we have covered the **areas** of agreement, where do scientists' opinions diverge?

2)____

____

In detail, the **theory**, as worked out over the years by other scientists, looks like this. The early atmosphere of the earth may have been composed of methane, ammonia, water, hydrogen sulfide, carbon dioxide or carbon monoxide and phosphate. Miller and Urey, in 1953, **demonstrated** that in such an atmosphere, a soup of basic organic molecules such as amino acids can be catalyzed by electrical activity. According to proponents of the chemical soup **theory**, these then might have combined into ever-more-**complex compounds** such as proteins and organic polymers, **ultimately** forming cells with self-replicating DNA. Unfortunately, this **process** both contains certain **contradictions** and has never been proved in any experimental activity, so **researchers** have spent much time putting forth many competing sub-**hypotheses**, including the deep sea vent **theory**, the iron-sulfur world **theory**, and the radioactive beach **theory**, trying to explain it. Although in its **variants** the **chemical** soup **hypothesis** is the most widely-accepted **theory**, there are others that compete with it, including clay **theory**.

Clay crystals can be widely **distributed** by wind and water. As these crystals grow, they tend to reproduce other crystals of the same shape, which can mutate depending upon their **external environment**. Dr. A. Graham Cairns-Smith postulated that these intricate crystals could have trapped organic molecules on their surfaces. These trapped molecules then increased in **complexity** when the clay crystals themselves increased in **complexity.** **Eventually**, these **complex** molecules trapped on the surface of the clay molecules could have performed a "genetic takeover" from their clay "**vehicle**," becoming **capable** of self-replication. In this way, 3)____________________

____

Recently, however, other experimenters have **found** fault with the idea that clay crystals could "**evolve**" in such a **complex** matter. Fortunately, Thomas Gold has another, perhaps more compelling, **theory**.

4)____

____

Support for his **theory** comes from two pieces of **evidence**. First, microbial life is known to be plentiful up to five kilometers below the surface of the earth. Also, nanobes (tiny **structures** smaller than bacteria, but perhaps containing DNA) have been discovered in deep rocks. Gold **theorized** that life began under the surface of the Earth because food from a deep, unreachable **source** was needed as life in an organic puddle would have exhausted its food **source** and become extinct. While Gold believed methane could have provided such a food **source**, other scientists now believe that hydrogen was the more likely **source**. If microbial life is **found** below the surface of another planet in our solar system, it will lead even more credence to Gold's **theory**.

The **final theory** to be explored here is also related to space. 5)________
____

Organic **compounds** are fairly common in the outer solar system. Comets are covered by a complex organic material formed from carbon **compounds** irradiated by ultraviolet light, and it is thought that their **impact** could have brought large quantities of this organic material to Earth. On the other hand, some **researchers** believe that life may have **evolved** more quickly on Mars, due to its smaller size and farther distance from the Sun. Asteroid and comet **impacts** perhaps then blasted this material off the surface of Mars and **transferred** it to Earth. Unfortunately, these **theories** do not explain how life first came about, but they offer the advantage that life was not **required** to originate on each planet separately, only once in the solar system.

There are more **theories** trying to explain abiogenesis than those presented here. Probably, future scientists will advance new **theories** regarding this question, and **abandon** some of those presented here. Perhaps they will find **conclusive** proof. Until then, followers of modern science are left in the perhaps uncomfortable position of being the only humans in history to not have a certain idea of where we came from.

Student B

Scientific **Controversies**: Information Gap

1. Student B, stay here. Student A, go to page 79.
2. The words and phrases are from the article below. Read them to your **partner** so that she can match them with the **definitions** she has.
3. Match your **definitions** with the words your **partner** provides

molecule	self-replicating	crystal	microbe	catalyze

a) __________ characteristic of a very early stage of development

b) __________ of, related to, or characteristic of living things

c) __________ the part of the world in which life can exist

d) __________ the air surrounding the earth

e) __________ any one of numerous nitrogen-containing acids from which proteins are made

Reading Strategy | Attributing Ideas

Task 5-3 We can use these expressions to report somebody else's opinion or findings. Go back through the **text** to find the original sentence in which they appeared and write them out.

________________ stated that ________________

According to ________________________________

________________ postulated that ________________

________________ **theorized** that ________________

________________ believe that ________________

Reading Strategy | The Language of Uncertainty

We use these **modal** verbs to **indicate** that an idea or fact is uncertain.

Past - could have/might have/may have/perhaps
Present - can/may/might/perhaps
Future –perhaps/probably/might

Task 5-4

Look through the article, "How Did We Get Here?" Circle the expressions above where you find them, and underline the sentences in which they are **found**. Compare your answers with a **partner**.

Comprehension Questions

Task 5-5

1. **Define** abiogenesis.
2. What four **theories** are outlined in this report?
3. Upon what two points do most **researchers** into the origin of life agree?
4. Which **chemicals** made up earth's early atmosphere?
5. According to the **chemical** soup **hypothesis**, how did self-replicating life come to exist? It is possible to simplify this explanation by using a flow chart like the one below. Finish it.

Early atmosphere composed of chemicals	⇨		⇨		⇨	

6. Explain the **concept** of "genetic takeover" in the clay **theory** model. You may find it useful to make a flow chart **similar** to the one above.
7. What problems exist for both the **chemical** soup **hypothesis** and the clay **theory** model?
8. What **evidence** supports Thomas Gold's deep, hot biosphere model?
9. What question does the extraterrestrial origin of life **theory** leave unanswered?
10. Among the four **theories** presented, which does the **author** believe is most probable? How do you know this?

Reaction Questions

Task 5-6

Discuss the following questions with a **partner**.

1. Do you think any of the **theories** above are probable? Is there any other **theory** of abiogenesis with which you agree?
2. What do you know about the formation of the Earth, solar system, or universe?
3. Do you know of any other scientific **controversies**? Explain one.
4. Write one more question that you would like to ask your **partner**.

   ▶ ____

5. Write 100 to 150 words on either of the questions above. Include five words from the **Academic** Word List, **highlighted** in bold.

Sentence Building: **Independent and Dependent Clauses**

A **clause** is a group of words that contains a subject and a verb. There are two kinds of **clauses** in English: independent **clauses** and dependent **clauses**.

Independent **clause**	life in an organic puddle would have exhausted its food **source**
Dependent **clause**	because life in an organic puddle would have exhausted its food **source**

- An independent **clause** has one subject-verb combination and expresses a complete thought. It can be a sentence by itself.

  The **chemical** soup **hypothesis** is the most widely-accepted **theory**.

- A dependent **clause** is an independent **clause** with a **subordinating** conjunction added to the beginning of it.

  although the **chemical** soup **hypothesis** is the most widely-accepted **theory**,

- A dependent **clause** does not express a complete thought, so it is not a sentence by itself. It needs to be joined to an independent **clause** to make a sentence.

Dependent **Clause** / Independent **Clause**

Although the **chemical** soup **hypothesis** is the most widely-accepted **theory**, there are others that compete with it.

- Use a comma (,) if the dependent **clause** comes first, but not if the independent **clause** comes first.

Since the Earth itself is thought to be about 5.5 billion years old, life appeared relatively early in the history of the planet.

Life appeared relatively early in the history of the planet since the Earth itself is thought to be about 5.5 billion years old.

Subordinating Conjunctions

There are many **subordinating** conjunctions. Some introduce reasons, some introduce times, and others introduce **contrast** and concessions. Here is a list of some of the **subordinating** conjunctions that we have seen so far, **plus** other important ones.

Time	**Condition**	**Purpose**	**Reason**	**Contrast**
after	as if	in order that	as	even though
as soon as	even if	so that	because	although
before	if		since	while
until	unless			
while	as long as			
when	when			
whenever				

Task 5-7

Work with a **partner**. Look back through the articles at the beginning of each chapter and circle as many of the subordinating conjunctions as you can find. Underline the sentences in which you find them. You have ten minutes. Who can find more?

Task 5-8

Fill in the blanks in the sentences below with a correct **subordinating** conjunction from the list above, using the words in brackets as guides. There may be more than one correct answer.

1. In Britain, a **debate** regarding fertility treatments has arisen ____________ (reason) reproductive **technology** is advancing very quickly.
2. ____________ (contrast) the **creation** of artificial human eggs and sperm is a realistic possibility in the near future, governments need to be very careful about allowing such **procedures**.
3. ____________ (condition) stem cell **technology** one day allows scientists to cultivate sperm or eggs from other parts of the body, infertile people could one day have children that are genetically their own.
4. This may be acceptable, ____________ (contrast) more **controversial procedures** such as two women having a child with no biological father are also possible.
5. Another **controversy** has been what happens to frozen embryos, eggs or sperm __________ (time) a **couple** has broken up.
6. A man might not want to father a child __________ (contrast) a women might believe that the embryos might be her last chance of a baby.
7. ____________ (purpose) the **welfare** of the future child is **considered**, fertility clinics must now **consider** the **commitment** of the parents to raising the children.
8. ____________ (reason) so many different strong beliefs are held by so many people, there will probably never be complete agreement on these **topics**.

Task 5-9

Combine a clause from column A with a clause from column B and write them as a paragraph in the space which follows. Be sure to punctuate them correctly.

A

1. Many South Koreans believe that a fan, if left running overnight in a closed room
2. According to the Korea **Consumer** Protection Board, if sleepers are **exposed** to an electric fan for too long
3. It is also possible to die from the increase of carbon dioxide and the decrease of oxygen
4. In order to guard against this possibility
5. Newspapers routinely report on the **phenomenon**, **citing** cases when victims die
6. Even though belief in this **phenomenon** is **widespread** in Korea
7. For example, Gord Giesbrecht, an **expert** on hypothermia, said it would be **virtually** impossible for someone to die of fan death,
8. Dr. John Linton of Severance Hospital says, although death from **exposure** to a fan is a common belief
9. Dr. Lee Yoon-song of Seoul National University has examined some of the victims and **found** that they had actually died
10. He said that if a Western doctor reported these deaths, he would say what really caused them

B

a) although a fan was beside the victim.

b) it is unknown outside the country,and many foreigners think it an urban myth.

c) can kill those **exposed** to it.

d) fans in South Korea come **equipped** with a timer.

e) because that person's body temperature could not drop by the **required** 10ºC overnight through the use of a fan alone.

f) it causes them to lose water and causes hypothermia.

g) other causes of death such as heart attacks or strokes were much more likely.

h) while a person is directly in **contact** with the air current from a fan.

i) after they fall asleep in their rooms with electric fans on.

j) since they had **underlying** problems such as heart disease or severe alcoholism.

Fan Death: Fact or Legend?

Writing Strategy | Summary

In **academic** writing, students are often called upon to **summarize** articles, **chapters** or ideas. This can be a difficult and tedious **process** for those who do not know how to **summarize** effectively or efficiently. This guide is intended to help you become acquainted with the **major** skills and pitfalls **involved** in **summarizing**.

In particular, you will learn how to take a composition of about 2 pages and reduce it to a one-**paragraph summary**.

Plagiarism

Taking another's words or ideas and using them as your own is a serious **academic** offence known as plagiarism. You must avoid directly **quoting** from your **source** without **acknowledgement**. Common sanctions for plagiarism include a "0" on your paper, failure of the course, or even expulsion from the university.

Citing the Source

When a student uses another's ideas, he must **acknowledge** where he **found** those ideas. Commonly, in a **summary**, the student will state in the first sentence the name of the **author** and the article that she is **summarizing**. Look at the **paragraph** below for an example.

Example **Paragraph**

We Come From Where?

In his article, "How Did We Get Here?" Robert Jeens outlines some of the **major theories** regarding abiogenesis, or the origin of life upon Earth. **Initially**, he looks at the **chemical** soup **hypothesis**. This most popular **theory** states that life came to be in an ancient, oxygen-free atmosphere, in which very simple organic **compounds** were formed, which then metabolized into more **complex compounds**, **ultimately** forming DNA-containing, self-replicating cells. The next **theory** he examines is clay **theory**, which **postulates** that organic molecules **evolved** in **complexity** by "piggybacking" on intricate and **complex** clay molecules, which provided a kind of **framework** for their development. Third, Thomas Gold stated that life originated several kilometers under the surface of the earth, feeding on deep, replenishable food **sources**. Last, some believe that life on Earth originally came from space. Jeens admits that these **theories** are just a few among many, and points out that modern scientists may be the first people to concede that we really don't know where we come from.

Finding the **Main Ideas :** Reducing the **Volume**

Obviously, when you **summarize**, you want to **transfer** only the most important ideas of the **author** and reduce the amount of writing **involved**. The length of your **summary** will **vary** from **project** to **project**, but the length of the **summary** for this project, one **paragraph**, is very common.

The following **method** will not work for every **summary**, but it is a good beginning. First, find the main idea of the entire essay. This main idea will probably be **located** in the first **paragraph** of the essay. Paraphrase the main idea and use it for the **topic** sentence of your **summary paragraph**. Next, look for the main ideas presented in the rest of the essay. Perhaps these main ideas will be represented in the topic sentences of the individual paragraphs in the composition you wish to summarize. Allow one sentence per main idea in your **summary**. Be sure to delete redundant or supporting information such as examples. **Finally**, **summarize** the **concluding paragraph** of the article in the **concluding** sentence of your **paragraph**.

You should not **insert** your own opinion into a **summary**. If you wish to state your opinion, that would go into another **paragraph** and is beyond the **scope** of this practice. Remember to leave your opinion out of a **summary paragraph**

Task 5-10

Compare the **topic** sentence of the example **paragraph** to the **thesis** statement of the article. Next, compare each sentence in the **paragraph** with the **corresponding paragraph** in the article. What do you notice?

Summary Paragraph Organization
Title
Topic Sentence includes: 1) main idea of the article, 2) name of the author of the article, 3) name of the article.
Body includes most important points that support the main idea of the article.
Concluding Sentence brings the paragraph to an end.

Quotation Marks

You may only **quote** directly from the article if you use **quotation** marks (“”), and you may only do this sparingly, perhaps once or twice in the entire **paragraph**. If you **quote** without **quotation** marks, it is a plagiarism. Follow these rules when using **quotation** marks.

1. Commas usually separate out a **quotation** from the rest of the sentence.
2. Use question marks (?) and exclamation points (!) as they naturally **occur** in the source.
3. Use a capital letter in the first letter of your **quotation** if it begins a sentence. Do not use a capital letter if it is not the beginning of a sentence

Task 5-11

The following information has been **quoted** directly from the article on pages 81 to 83. Rewrite the sentences using proper capitalization and punctuation. The first has been done for you.

1. aleksandr oparin claimed that a soup of organic molecules was **created** in Earth's primitive oxygen-free atmosphere

   *Alexander Oparin claimed, "that a soup of organic molecules was **created** in Earth's primitive, oxygen-free atmosphere."*

2. life developed several kilometers under the surface of the earth or so thomas gold believed

   ▶ ______________________________

   ____

3. while gold postulated that methane could have provided such a food **source** through further **research** other scientists now believe that hydrogen was the more likely **source**

⊙ ______________________________

____

4. because of its smaller size and farther distance from the sun life may have begun on mars first

⊙ ______________________________

____

5. the fact that modern scientists are the only humans in history to not have a certain idea of where we came from seems to be an uncomfortable reality

⊙ ______________________________

____

Paraphrasing

Paraphrasing is another key to reducing plagiarism. When you paraphrase, you take another's ideas, keep the meaning, but express the ideas in your own words so that you do not plagiarize. Paraphrasing can be done at the level of the **paragraph**, but it is useful to learn how to do it for **individual** sentences first. Three tips for effective paraphrasing are: 1) switch from **passive** to active **tense** or active to **passive tense**, 2) switch dependent and independent **clauses**, and, most importantly, 3) keep **technical** vocabulary while changing regular vocabulary.

• Switching from Passive to Active

Most sentences are in the active **tense** (subject + verb + object), so switching them to the **passive tense** (object + verb + by + subject) can be a way to paraphrase effectively.

(Subject) + *verb* + [object]

(Asteroid and comet **impacts**) perhaps then *blasted* [this material] off the surface of Mars.

Can be changed to:

This material then perhaps *was blasted* off the surface of Mars by (asteroid and comet **impacts**.)

Alternatively, you can change a **passive** sentence to the active tense.

Comets *are covered* by (a **complex** organic material.)

Can be changed to:

(A **complex** organic material) covers comets

• Switching Dependent and Independent Clauses

Another **method** for good paraphrasing is to switch the order of dependent and independent **clauses**. Switch the **subordinating** conjunction for another with a **similar** meaning.

(**Subordinating** conjunction) + *dependent **clause*** + independent **clause**

*(Although) in its **variants** the **chemical** soup **hypothesis** is the most widely-accepted **theory**,* there are others that compete with it.

Can be changed to:

There are other **theories** that compete with the **chemical** soup **hypothesis** (even though) *it is the most widely accepted.*

• Keeping Technical Vocabulary and Changing Regular Vocabulary

In most **academic** papers, some vocabulary is very **precise** and **technical**, so that there is no **substitute** for it. However, many words can be **substituted** for others of **similar** meanings. Look at the following example.

Comets are covered by a **complex** organic material formed from carbon **compounds** irradiated by ultraviolet light.

Can be changed to:

Comets are surrounded by a complicated organic substance made from carbon **compounds altered** by ultraviolet light.

Task 5-12

Paraphrase the following sentences. Use the **techniques** outlined above, including changing from active to **passive tense** or from **passive** to active **tense**, changing the order of dependent and independent **clauses**, and keeping **technical** vocabulary and changing regular vocabulary.

1. First proposed in 1924, Aleksandr Oparin's **chemical** soup **theory** stated that a soup of organic molecules was **created** in Earth's primitive, oxygen-free atmosphere through the action of sunlight and lightning.
   *Sunlight and lightning **interacted** with Earth's early, anaerobic atmosphere to make a mixture of organic molecules, according to Alexanr Oparin's 1924 **chemical** soup **theory**.*
2. At the moment, there is very little agreement among scientists to one of the central questions of existence: abiogenesis, or the origin of life on Earth.
   ▶ ______________________________

   ____
3. Since the Earth itself is thought to be about 5.5 billion years old and was unsuitable for life for the first 500 to 800 million years, life appeared relatively early in the history of the planet.
   ▶ ______________________________

   ____
4. While Gold believed methane could have provided such a food **source**, other scientists now believe that hydrogen was the more likely **source**.
   ▶ ______________________________

   ____
5. Probably, future scientists will advance new **theories** regarding this question, and **abandon** some of those presented here.
   ▶ ______________________________

   ____

Academic Vocabulary Development

Task 5-13 **Adjectives 2**

You must put the word that follows the sentence into its correct adjectival form and use it to fill in the blank in the sentence. Check these sentences with the original sentences from the **text** to see how different word forms are used.

1. Although ____________, the boundaries of ecoregions blend into each other. (**distinctiveness**) (61)
2. This statement is ____________ of the fact that, at the moment, there is very little agreement among scientists to one of the central questions of existence. (**illustrates**) (81)
3. What modern science offers are several competing, perhaps-____________ models. (**validity**) (81)
4. Unfortunately, this **process** both contains certain ____________ **assumptions** and has never been proved in any experimental activity. (**contradictions**) (82)
5. These **complex** molecules trapped on the surface of the clay molecules could have become organic and performed an ____________ "genetic takeover" from their clay "**vehicle**." (**eventually**) (82)
6. Unfortunately, there is no ____________ support for how life first came about in outer space. (**theories**) (83)
7. Although artificially-____________ human eggs and sperm are realistic possibilities in the near future, governments need to be very careful about allowing such **procedures**. (**creation**) (89)
8. Another ____________ **topic** has been what happens to frozen embryos, eggs or sperm after a **couple** has broken up. (**controversy**) (89)
9. The length of your **summary** will be ____________ from **project** to **project**. (**vary**) (93)
10. Use naturally-____________ question marks and exclamation points from the **source**. (**occur**) (95)

Academic Writing **Assignment**: **Summarize** an Article

Choose one of the following reading passages and **summarize** it in one **paragraph**. Follow the **guidelines** that have been presented in this **chapter**. Use at least five words from the **Academic** Word List that have appeared in the book so far. Type the words in bold so that your teacher can easily identify them.

- **Chapter** 1: Regenerative **Medicine**
- **Chapter** 3: The International Space Station
- **Chapter** 4: Ecoregions of Korea

Summary Paragraph Checklist

Form

- Does the **paragraph** use correct **paragraph** form?
- Are there 8 to 12 sentences?

Organization

- Does the **topic** sentence of the **paragraph** include the author of the article's name, the name of the article and the main idea of the essay being **summarized**?
- Have effective **summarizing techniques** been used and plagiarism avoided?
- Is there an effective **concluding** sentence?

Content

- Does the **paragraph** engage the reader's interest in the title and **topic** sentence?
- Is the **paragraph** direct and **clear**?
- Does the **paragraph** use **appropriate** vocabulary?
- Does the **paragraph** use a variety of sentence **structures** to make the **paragraph** more interesting?
- Does the body contain the most important details of the essay?
- Has opinion been avoided?
- Are there five words from the **Academic** World List in bold?

Grammar and Mechanics

- Does the writer avoid mistakes of spelling, capitalization and punctuation?
- Are there any mistakes of singular or plural?
- Does the writer avoid sentence fragments?
- Does the writer use correct verb **tenses**?
- Are conjunctions used correctly?
- Do the nouns, pronouns and verbs agree with each other?
- Are prepositional phrases used correctly?
- Are noun, verb, adjective and adverb forms used correctly?

Chapter

06 Korean Education

English Education Questionnaire

1. Look at the questions below and think about your answers.
2. Ask your **partner** the questions, record her answer, and give your answers.
3. Be prepared to discuss your answers with the class.

---

1. What **percentage** of students graduate from high school in Korea (take a guess)?
2. a) How do you think Korean students compare in mathematics, science and reading to their international peers?

   b) Why is this?
3. What was your parents opinion of the schools you attended?
4. What, in your opinion, are the strengths and weaknesses of the Korean educational system?

Scrambled Words

Task 6-1

These words are from the article below. Unscramble them and match them with their **definitions**.

1. noctnet 2. knar 3. racylite
4. papraisla 5. eaiaiagltrn 6. satisdisfaction

a) _________ the position of something in an order or **sequence**
b) _________ the idea that all people should be equal
c) _________ the **elements** of which something **consists**
d) _________ not pleased or not content
e) _________ the ability to read and write
f) _________ an official **assessment** of the strengths and weaknesses of something

OECD Education at a Glance: What Does it Tell Us about Korean Education?

The Organization for **Economic Cooperation** and Development **annually** tracks and compares the progress of students in its member countries. This Program for International Student **Assessment** is a valuable tool for member countries to discover the relative performances of their educational systems. **Significantly**, it measures student performance, the learning **environment**, teacher and parent **perceptions**, and the **role** of the private **sector** versus public **funding**. By looking at these **factors**, we can see the Korean educational system's real strengths and important weaknesses.

Firstly, student **achievement** in Korea is near the top of the pack. In 2007, Korea had a high school graduation rate of 91%, which put it in eighth place, above the OECD average of 87%. Also, the quality of learning students engaged in was very high. Korean 15-year-olds ranked well above the OECD average in scientific literacy: in tenth place **overall**. Korean students ranked second in mathematical literacy, and, most impressively, Korean students were ranked number one in reading literacy. Even more, this **achievement** is more egalitarian than in other countries. 23% of "top performers" in science, mathematics and reading came from a socioeconomic background below the OECD average, a record topped by only five countries. As they **approach** the end of secondary school, Korean students seem well-prepared for university.

When the **survey** compares the learning **environments** across the OECD, the Korean case presents several difficult-to-explain **trends**. First, there is a superior **investment** in education. Education spending accounted for 7.3% of Korea's **economy**, behind only Iceland, Israel and the United States. The OECD average was 6.1%. However, the number of actual instructional hours was the third lowest in the OECD. Between the ages of 7 and 14, Korean students spend less than 6,000 hours in the classroom, compared to an OECD average of 6,850 hours. Also, under 80% of this time was spent on actual teaching and learning, rather than keeping order or **administrative** tasks, which is below the OECD average. Lastly, with an average of over 30 students per class as opposed to an OECD average of 22, Korean classrooms are the largest in the OECD. There is a large **investment** in education and Korean students perform well **despite** being in large classrooms for a relatively short amount of time. What about teachers?

The **assessment** of teachers in Korea is problematic. Korean teachers are more frequently **evaluated** than their peers in the OECD: 56% of Korean teachers are **evaluated** at least **annually**, compared to 45% in the OECD. However, 91% believed that this appraisal was neither a fair **assessment** of their work as a teacher, nor was it helpful in the development of their work as teachers, and 60% said the **evaluation** was done only to fulfill an

administrative requirement. Again, 88% said that they would receive no reward for improving the quality of their teaching, and 90% reported that teachers would not be fired because of poor performance. It seems that teachers are generally dissatisfied with the **methods** used to **evaluate** them.

Korean parents, too, were relatively unsatisfied with the public education system. They placed sixth out of ten countries in their **responses** to two questions, "I am satisfied with the disciplinary atmosphere in my child's school," and "School does a good job in educating students." They placed seventh out of ten when asked, "I am happy with the content taught and **instructional methods** used in school." **Finally**, Korean parents ranked ninth of ten in their **responses** to "Standards of **achievement** in school are high" and "Most of the teachers in school seem competent and dedicated." What is the **response** of parents to this general dissatisfaction?

Korean parents **invest** in private education. In fact, Korea has the largest **proportion** of private educational **investment** in the OECD, at 41.2%. The OECD average was 15.3%. There is a vast, **parallel** system of private educational **institutes** that offer **supplementary**, after-school classes in everything from mathematics to science to English to art. After a school day which their parents pretty much regard as time wasted, Korean students go to the places where they do their real learning: **institutes**. Students' high scores compared to the rest of the world are the result not of **instruction** that they have received in public schools, but in the private educational system **financed** directly by their parents.

The good news is that, in Korea, students are learning. Their high ranking internationally is proof of that. Unfortunately, the OECD report **implies** that the public educational system needs change. Class sizes need to be made smaller, students need more **instruction**, and the system needs to **respond** to the general dissatisfaction of parents and teachers that has seen students flee to the **supplementary** private educational system.

Reading Strategy | Making a Mind Map

We introduced the **concept** of "clustering" in **Chapter** 1 as a way of **generating** and organizing ideas for writing. Mind mapping is very **similar** to clustering, but in **reverse**. Rather than using it as a **method** for writing, mind mapping allows a student to **analyze** the content and **structure** of a composition. Mind maps also hold information in a **format** that your mind will find easy to remember and quick to review. Rather than just listing the information in a composition, mind maps show the "shape" of a subject, the relative importance of **individual** points, and the way in which facts relate to each other.

Task 6-2

On the next page is a partially completed mind map for the article above. Complete it.

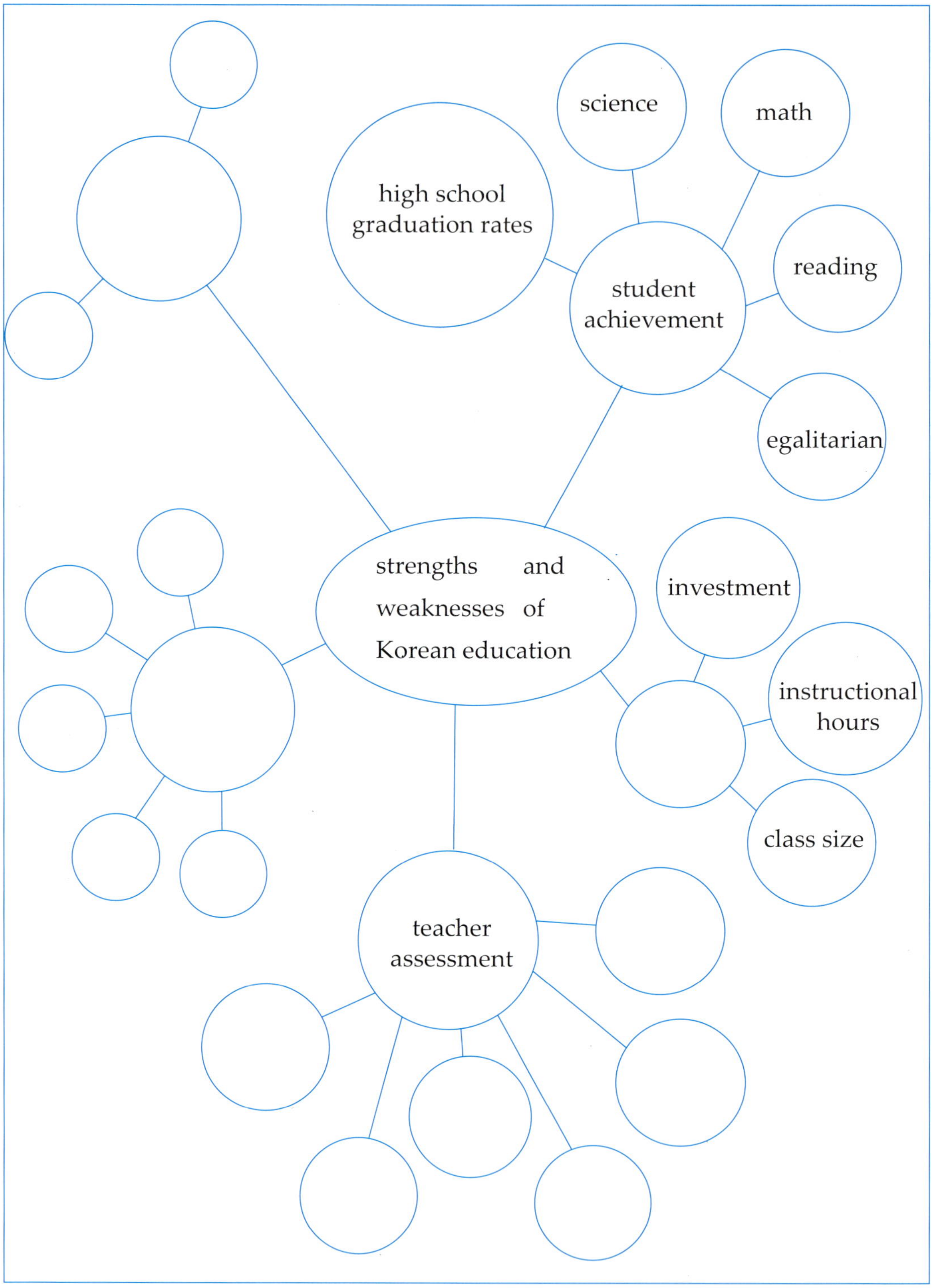
strengths and weaknesses of Korean education
high school graduation rates
student achievement
science
math
reading
egalitarian
investment
instructional hours
class size
teacher assessment

Comprehension Questions

Task 6-3

1. What does the author want to do?
   a) describe the Korean education system.
   b) compare the Korean education system to its OECD peers.
   c) measure student performance in Korea.
   d) **summarize** "Education at a Glance."

2. What five **factors** will the **author investigate**?

3. Write the correct **statistic** next to each **factor**.
   a) __________ high school graduation rate
   b) __________ ranking in science
   c) __________ ranking in math
   d) __________ ranking in reading
   e) __________ ranking in egalitarianism

4. What **contradiction** does the third paragraph present?

5. Why are Korean teachers dissatisfied with the **methods** used to **evaluate** them?

6. What are the two most serious **sources** of parental dissatisfaction with the education system in Korea?

7. What is the result of parental dissatisfaction with the education system?

8. What recommendations does the **author** make?

Reaction Questions

Task 6-4

Discuss the following questions with a **partner**.

1. Do you agree or disagree with the **author**'s **assessment** of the Korean education system?

2. Describe a **positive**, memorable learning experience that you have had.

3. Who has been your best or worst teacher? Why do you say that?

4. Write one more question that you would like to ask your **partner** about the **topic**.

   ▶ ______________________________

5. Write 100 to 150 words on either of the questions above. Include five words from the **Academic** Word List, **highlighted** in bold..

Writing Skill — From Paragraph to Essay

While a **paragraph** is usually about one **aspect** of a **topic**, an essay allows a writer to broaden and deepen the **topic**. Let's begin by **analyzing** the **structure** of a typical essay by comparing it to the **structure** of a **paragraph**.

Paragraph	Essay
Topic Sentence • includes main idea of the **paragraph** and has a controlling idea	**Introductory Paragraph** • gets the reader's attention and includes the **thesis** statement of the essay
Body • includes supporting sentences and details	**Body** • includes supporting **paragraphs**, each with its own **topic** sentence and **concluding** sentence
Concluding Sentence • **reinforces** main idea and leaves the reader with a strong impression	**Concluding Paragraph** • **reinforces** main idea and leaves the reader with a strong impression

Example Essay

Snow White and the Seven Professors

Introductory Paragraph A

Snow White had seven dwarves. **Likewise**, there are seven types of professors: Happy, Dopey, Doc, Sneezy, Sleepy, Bashful, and Grumpy. Surprised?

Introductory Paragraph B

There are fairy tales in every **culture**. America has the tooth fairy, Europe has Cinderella, and Korea has Kongji. These stories have universal **relevance** as they **display cultural themes** and archetypes. The characters in the stories have personalities in **evidence** all over the world. In universities, this can be seen by a comparison of Snow White's dwarves and professors. Just as Snow White had seven dwarves, there are seven types of professors; they are Happy, Dopey, Doc, Sneezy, Sleepy, Bashful, or Grumpy.

Most students like it when they have a Happy Professor. He comes into the classroom smiling, leaves smiling, and makes a lot of jokes during the class. He is a very nice man, so that everyone feels good. Happy, nice: what's the problem? The problem is that you may not learn much from him. In that way, the Happy Professor is very **similar** to the next type.

The Dopey Professor forgets many things. She is often late for class, and then has forgotten to bring her notes. Where is the attendance sheet? What is your name? What is her name? What are we talking about? How did she ever get to be a professor? She doesn't know.

"Doc" is always asking about your absences from class. Were you sick? What was wrong? Did you take any **medicine**? Do you have a doctor's note? He has become an **expert** in diagnosing sick students. He suspects you had "hookyitis," so he believes that the best medicine is always attending class.

On the other hand, the Sneezy Professor is always sick herself. She often cancels class, and when she is present, she is weak. Sometimes, she gets other professors to **substitute** for her. She is probably too old to really work, but here she is. If you like to have few classes, this is the professor for you.

Another type of professor who **constantly** misses classes, or is often late, is the Sleepy Professor. He just can't get out of bed in the morning, so he is often late for his first class. When he has a break between classes, he sleeps in his office. Don't visit him there, or you will wake him up. When he is in class, he yawns a lot, or, sometimes, he sleeps right through class. The Sleepy Professor may be close to retirement.

Conversely, the Bashful Professor is very new. This is her first class, and she is extremely nervous. You see her hands shake as she clenches her notes, her trembling voice barely rising above the din of students in **conversation**, **ignoring** her. She is very happy to meet you, but scared of all the students in class. Some day, she may be confident and in control, but not yet.

The Grumpy Professor is **definitely** confident and in control; too confident and too in control. He never smiles. You walk in two minutes late, and he yells at you. He thinks students today are lazy and stupid, and you are the laziest and stupidest he has ever seen. He often tells you this. You are not entitled to an opinion yet; his are all that matter. Do you belong at this university? You probably don't.

Concluding Paragraph A

Some people may find it amusing that their professors resemble the Seven Dwarves: Happy, Dopey, Doc, Sneezy, Sleepy, Bashful and Grumpy.

Concluding Paragraph B

Some people may find it amusing that their professors resemble the Seven Dwarves: Happy, Dopey, Doc, Sneezy, Sleepy, Bashful and Grumpy. Perhaps all people in the world could be compared to fairy tale characters. That may be one of the things that give fairy tales their universal relevance. From Pinocchio to the Big Bad Wolf, the mythical characters display very human traits.

Task 6-5

Although the body of the essay is the same, there are two introductory and **concluding paragraphs** to **illustrate** two of the most common types. Fill in the essay outline below to learn more.

Plain Introductory Paragraph (A)

•Why is introductory paragraph A called a "plain introductory paragraph?"

Funnel Introductory Paragraph (B)

• Why is introductory paragraph B called a "funnel introductory paragraph?"

Paragraph 2
Topic Sentence
Concluding Sentence
(**transition**?)

Paragraph 3
Topic Sentence
Concluding Sentence
(**transition**?)

Paragraph 4
Topic Sentence
Concluding Sentence
(**transition**?)

Paragraph 5
Topic Sentence
Concluding Sentence
(**transition**?)

Paragraph 6
Topic Sentence
Concluding Sentence
(**transition**?)

Paragraph 7
Topic Sentence
Concluding Sentence
(**transition**?)

Paragraph 8
Topic Sentence
Concluding Sentence
(**transition**?)

Plain Introductory Paragraph (A)

- Why is concluding paragraph A called a "plain concluding paragraph?"

Triangle **Concluding Paragraph**

- Why is **concluding paragraph** B called a "triangle **concluding paragraph**?"

Essay Organization

The Introductory Paragraph

Every introductory **paragraph** has two main **functions**. First, it should catch the attention of the reader and make her want to keep reading. Second, it must contain the **thesis** statement or the main idea of the essay. There are many ways to do this. We will examine three here.

Plain Introduction

This is the easiest and sometimes a very effective **method**. Simply state the **thesis** statement plainly, and perhaps add a sentence or two to **link** it to the first **paragraph**. Introductory **paragraph** A in the example essay above is a plain introduction.

Funnel Introduction

This introduction goes from a general statement about the **topic**, and then gradually narrows the subject throughout the **paragraph** to end with the **thesis** statement. Look at introductory **paragraph** B to see how a funnel introduction is **structured**

Problem-Solution Introduction

This introduction introduces a problem, to which the writer offers a solution in the **thesis** statement at the end of the introductory **paragraph**. Look at the introductory **paragraph** in the first reading in **Chapter** 5, "How Did We Get Here?" for an example of a problem-solution introduction. What is the problem? What is the solution?

The Body of an Essay

The body of an essay **consists** of a series of **paragraphs**, each with its own **topic** sentence, body and **concluding** sentence.

The ideas in the **paragraphs** are **linked** together by **transition** sentences and expressions. Not every **paragraph** needs to be **linked** to every other **paragraph**, but several should be. There are three main **methods** to **link** these **paragraphs**.

- **Concluding Sentence as a Transition Sentence**

  A writer can use the **concluding** sentence of a **paragraph** to look forward to the subject of the next **paragraph**.

  In that way, the Happy Professor is very similar to the next type.

- **Topic Sentence as a Transition Sentence**

  A writer can use the **topic** sentence of a **paragraph** to **summarize** the **preceding paragraph** in order to show a continuity of ideas.

  Another type of professor who misses many classes, or is often late, is the Sleepy Professor.

- **Transition Expressions in the Topic Sentence**

  We have already looked at some **transition** expressions as they are used to **link** ideas within **paragraphs**. In addition, a writer can **insert** a **transition** expression in the **topic** sentence of a **paragraph** to **link** the ideas in two **paragraphs**.

  On the other hand, the Sneezy Professor is always sick herself.

Transition Expressions

Here is a partial list of **transition** expressions.

Relationship	Examples
addition	in addition, also, moreover, **furthermore**, as well, what is more
comparison	**similarly**, in the same way, **likewise**
concession	certainly, of course, to be sure, no doubt
consequence	therefore, thus, as a result, as a **consequence**, for this reason
contrast	however, on the **contrary**, on the other hand, in **contrast**
emphasis	above all, especially, indeed, in fact, in particular, surely
example	for example, for **instance**
restatement	in other words
sequence	afterwards, at last, at present, currently, **eventually**, **finally**,
summary	in **conclusion**, to **summarize**, in **summary**, all in all, to **sum** up

The **transition** expressions above are adverbial conjunctions. They are used in two different ways.

- We use these to begin a sentence and follow the adverbial conjunction with a comma.

  In addition, the true **goal** most Koreans have in mind when they study English is not **communication**.

- We can also use these in the middle of a sentence if they are **preceded** by a semicolon.

  A few native-speaker English teachers have been added; however, students are not **exposed** to them **consistently** enough for real progress.

Task 6-6

Work with a **partner**. Review the introductory readings at the beginning of each chapter. Circle the **transition** expressions you find. Underline the sentences in which they appear. You have ten minutes. Who can find more?

Task 6-7

Complete the following sentences to make a meaningful sentence.

1. Jill has been studying English for six years. Therefore, ________________________.
2. She is conscientious in most of her subjects. In the same way, ________________.
3. She prefers to use English naturally, and not worry about grammar too much. On the other hand, ________________.
4. Jill likes to chat on the Internet with foreign friends. In addition, ______________.
5. Sometimes, she has trouble understanding new words. For example, ___________.
6. **Overall**, she feels that she is fairly proficient at English. **Nevertheless**, __________.
7. In **conclusion**, ____.

The Concluding Paragraph

There are many different ways to **conclude** an essay. All **methods** try to leave the reader with a lasting impression of the essay. Usually, but not always, they also restate the **thesis** statement. We will look at three different types of **concluding paragraph**.

Plain Concluding Paragraph

In this type of **concluding paragraph**, the **author** simply restates the **thesis** statement in different words. While this is very simple, it can be very effective. Look at **concluding paragraph** A for an example of a plain **concluding paragraph**.

Triangle Concluding Paragraph.

In this type of **concluding paragraph**, the **author** moves from **specific** to general. Beginning with a narrow restatement of the **thesis** statement, it broadens out to draw general conclusions about society as a whole or some other larger situation from this **specific** state of affairs. Look at **concluding paragraph** B for an example of a triangle **concluding paragraph**.

Predictive Concluding Paragraph

In this type of **concluding paragraph**, the **author** looks to the possible future of the situation which the essay describes. The **author** could make **predictions**, call for future action by some **authority**, or outline different **scenarios**. Look at the **concluding paragraph** of the first essay in **Chapter** 6, "OECD Education at a Glance," for an example of a **predictive concluding paragraph**. What **predictions** or calls for action does the author make?

Sentence Building: **Articles (a, an, the)**

A, An: The Indefinite Article

We use the indefinite article:

- when we are introducing a singular, countable noun : a natural ability
- when we are talking about any one of many things : a recent **survey**
- in front of professions : a mechanic
- in front of expressions of quantity like : a *few*, *a little* a lot of, a great deal of
- instead of *one* or *per* when giving the rate or pace of something : a typhoon a summer

The: The Definite Article

We use the definite article:

- before a singular, countable or uncountable noun when both the reader and writer are familiar with the idea already : the story of the accidental discovery of penicillin
- to **indicate** something **specifically** : the large living quarters in the middle
- when there is only one of something : the popular IELTS test
- before the formal names of countries : the Republic of Korea
- before some superlatives : the stupidest Canadian
- before oceans, rivers, hotels, theaters, museums and newspapers : the Pacific Ocean, the Han River, the Westin Hotel, the Grand Theater, the Natural History Museum, the Korea Herald

No Article

We don't use an article:

- when we are introducing general ideas : **cultural** and educational barriers
- before common names of countries : Korea, America
- before towns, streets, languages, magazines, meals, airports, stations and mountains : Seoul, Sejong Street, Korean, Time, lunch, Kimpo Airport, Seoul Station, Mount Everest

• before some places and with some forms of **transportation** : at home, in/to bed, at/ to work, at/to school, by bus, by plane, by car, by train, on foot

Task 6-8

Write in the, a, an, or X in the blanks and check your answers in the essay above.

1. Most ____ students like it when they have ____ Happy Professor.
2. He comes into ____ classroom smiling, leaves smiling, and makes ____ lot of jokes during ____ class.
3. He is ____ very nice man, so that ____ everyone feels good.
4. ____ problem is that you may not learn much from him.
5. In that way, ____ Happy Professor is very **similar** to ____ next type.
6. ____ Dopey Professor forgets many things.
7. Where is ____ attendance sheet?
8. How did she ever get to be ____ professor?
9. "Doc" is always asking about your absences from ____ class.
10. Do you have ____ doctor's note?
11. He has become ____ **expert** in diagnosing sick students.
12. He suspects you had ____ "hookyitis," so, for him, ____ best **medicine** is always attending class.
13. On ____ other hand, ____ Sneezy Professor is always sick herself.

Task 6-9

All of the articles have been **removed** from the following article. You can see them in parentheses before each **paragraph**.

1. Split the class into groups and **assign** one paragraph to each group. Have the group place the articles in their correct positions.
2. **Assign** one member from each group to a new group so that they can finish the article.

Less Effort, Better Results

(a, the, the, the, the, the, the) In 2008, Koreans spent 15 trillion won on private English education. **Furthermore**, 97% of Korean office workers asked in recent **survey** if they felt need to study English more, answered, "Yes." Yet Koreans ranked 19th out of 20 countries in their scores on popular IELTS (International English Language Testing System) test. In tests, Korean applicants had especially poor **outcomes** in speaking and writing sections. What is going on here? **Despite** all time, effort and **stress**, why can't Koreans speak and write English better? Simple answer is that Koreans need to spend less time studying English and more time naturally using English.

(a, a, a, a, the, the, the, the, the) When I say "naturally using English," what do I mean? Language teaching **professionals** make **distinction** between knowledge about language and skill in using that language. Think about **difference** between being **mechanic** and having ability to drive well. Many of my students have spent lot of time learning about English grammar and vocabulary, but are not skilled at using that knowledge. They are like auto **mechanics** who can't drive. Most native speakers are just opposite; we drive very well, but often can't describe grammar in intellectual terms. Anyway, it seems that education system in Korea forces students to use their time poorly. Rather than learning skill of using English, students spend their precious time studying about English.

(a, a, a) Unfortunately, there are **cultural** and educational barriers to **implementing** this learning **process** in Korea. Learning language **requires** great deal of experimentation; it **requires** willingness to make mistakes in **construction** while searching for meaning. You need to be tolerant of **communication** breakdowns and not saying exactly what you want to say. Students must be vocal and active learners. Korea's school **culture** does not reward these traits. In class, students have been taught not to stand out from their peers. They are told that quiet students learn more than students who speak up and draw attention to themselves. Children who express opinions are treated as disruptive. Good speakers believe that **demonstrating** their skills in front of their poorer classmates will make those classmates feel bad, while the not-so-good speakers are ashamed to **display** their poor English skills. These **conventional** values are inimical to good language teaching and learning.

(a, a, a, the, the, the, the, the) In addition, **ultimate goal** most Koreans have in mind when they study English is not **communication**: it is passing of test. These tests control who will be admitted to which schools and companies, and so are **crucial** for success in modern, competitive Korean **economy**. Therefore, **strategies**, skills and knowledge necessary for excelling in test are far more important to them than **strategies**, skills and knowledge necessary for real **communication**. Under these **circumstances**, students follow strategy of real **communication** if necessary, but not necessarily real **communication**. How can students overcome these problematic **attitudes**?

(a, a, the, the, the) There are Korean students who have been inspired to learn foreign languages. Other people think they are gifted, and perhaps in some ways they are, but I find what really separates them from others is their **resolve** to **communicate** in English. While we are watching TV, reading or exercising, they are studying flash cards or chatting on Internet in language not their own. They are meeting foreign students, joining English clubs, and reading English books. They go to their professor's office just to speak, and meet their friends to read and discuss latest articles in Time. Not all excellent English speakers have been abroad. Good Korean English speakers have assiduously **sought** out every opportunity they could to **interact** in foreign language right here in this country **despite** all obstacles.

(a, a, a, an, the, the, the, the, the, the) There are both unfortunate and hopeful portents for future of this idea. Unfortunately, most high schools don't look like they will be changing their language teaching **strategies** any time soon. On other hand, some foreign-language, private and other experimental schools are beginning to introduce more actual speaking practice, and not just ceremonial once- -week session with inexperienced native speaker. Also, very few schools are beginning to experiment with more open **concepts** in teaching that lay at heart of encouraging **innovation** in language learning. Perhaps success that students from these schools will enjoy will encourage laggards to **shift** their **dominant** educational **paradigm**.

Academic Vocabulary Development

Task 6-10

Nouns 2

You must put the word that follows the sentence into its correct noun form and use it to fill in the blank in the sentence. Check these sentences with the original sentences from the **text** to see how different word forms are used.

1. Organic molecules **undergo** a **complex** __________. (**evolved**) (82)
2. Just under 80% of this time was spent on actual teaching and learning, as opposed to keeping order or __________. (**administrative**) (103)
3. 56% of Korean teachers have an **annual** __________. (**evaluated**) (104)
4. I am happy with the content taught and **methods** of __________ used in

school. (**instructional**) (104)

5. Korean parents have a large __________ in private education (**invest**) (104)
6. These stories have universal **relevance** as they **display themes** from many __________. (**cultural**) (109)
7. Sometimes, another professor comes in as a __________ for her. (**substitute**) (110)
8. Unfortunately, there are **cultural** and educational barriers to the __________ of this natural learning **process** in Korea. (**implementing**) (121)
9. A __________ of learning a language is a great deal of experimentation. (**requires**) (121)
10. Good Korean English speakers have assiduously **sought** out every opportunity they could for __________ in a foreign language right here in this country **despite** all the obstacles. (**interact**) (122)

Academic Writing Assignment: The Essay

Write a four to six **paragraph** essay on one of the following **topics**. Use at least five words from the **Academic** Word List that have appeared in the book so far.

1. I agree/disagree with the importance of the Korean University Entrance Examination.
2. Write about a **positive**, memorable learning experience that you have had.
3. Who was your best teacher ever?
4. What are the most important differences between high school and university?

The Writing Process

1. Get some ideas to write with. You can brainstorm, free write, cluster, or do **research**. You need reasons for your opinion and support for your reasons.
2. a) Organize your ideas into an essay outline. Put each of your reasons into a **paragraph** and organize your support in the **paragraph**.

   b) Look at the outline on pages 110 to 112 for an example. Which of the three

methods of introduction and **conclusion** will you use? Your **thesis** statement must be included in your introductory **paragraph**.

3. Write your first **draft**.
   a) Make sure all your **paragraphs** have **topic** and **concluding** sentences. The **topic** sentence will be your reason, and the body will be the support for your **topic** sentence. Most of the **paragraphs** should also have **transition** sentences.
   b) Check your grammar against the essay checklist below.
4. Write a **final**, 2-page essay to hand in to your teacher.

Essay Checklist
Form • Do the **paragraphs** use correct **paragraph** form? • Is the essay 4-6 **paragraphs** long with 12-point type?
Organization • Does the introductory **paragraph** include a **thesis** statement? • Does the **concluding paragraph** leave the reader with a lasting impression? • Do the **paragraphs** have **topic** sentences and **concluding** sentences? • Are there **transition** sentences? • Do all the ideas in the essay relate to the **thesis** statement? • Is there any redundancy?
Content • Do the title and introductory **paragraph** make the reader want to keep reading? • Is the essay language direct and **clear**? • Does the essay use **appropriate** vocabulary? • Does the essay use a variety of sentence **structures** to make it more interesting? • Does the body support the **thesis** statement well? • Are there at least five words from the **Academic** Word List in bold?
Grammar and Mechanics • Does the writer avoid mistakes of spelling, capitalization and punctuation? • Are there any mistakes of singular or plural? • Does the writer avoid sentence fragments? • Does the writer use correct verb **tenses**? • Are conjunctions used correctly? • Do the nouns, pronouns and verbs agree with each other? • Are prepositions used correctly? • Are noun, verb, adjective and adverb forms used correctly? • Are articles used correctly?

Chapter

07 The Korean Economy

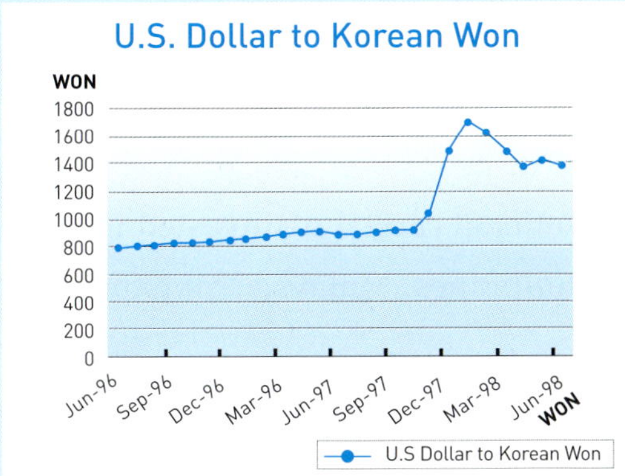

Look at the graph on the right with a **partner**.

a) What does it show?

b) What **period** of time does it cover?

c) What is the name of this event?

d) Can you explain the causes or effects of this event?

Task 7-1 Vocabulary

Match the words and phrases on the left with the **definitions** on the right.

1. _____ bankrupt
2. _____ capital
3. _____ a **creditor**
4. _____ a conglomerate
5. _____ default
6. _____ foreign **currency** reserves
7. _____ foreign exchange
8. _____ interest
9. _____ profit
10. _____ sovereign

a) unable to pay what you owe so that you must sell your property to pay your debts

b) fail to pay a debt that you **legally** owe

c) relating to a country or government

d) somebody to whom money is owed

e) a company that owns many businesses whose products or services are unrelated

f) wealth, especially money, or businesses, or property that can be sold to **generate** money

g) money charged by a bank for borrowing money

h) the system **whereby** the type of money in one country is exchanged for another country's money

i) to earn money from something

j) money a government keeps to pay its international debts in case of emergency

Transition Sentences Practice

Task 7-2

The sentences below are **transition** sentences. **Insert** them into the article below.

a) In **contrast** to the overdeveloped conglomerates, banks in Korea were underdeveloped and weak.

b) Such a **corporate** failure was about to happen.

c) This crisis became **regional** as international capital **disinvested** in not only Thailand, but also Indonesia, the Philippines, Malaysia, Singapore, Hong Kong, and, of course, Korea.

d) This Asia-wide **economic decline** would **impact** Korea's **unique** business model.

e) While this crisis was unfolding in Korea, what led to the immediate **collapse** was the devaluation of the Thai baht.

Korea and the Asian **Economic** Crisis of 1997

Companies went bankrupt or were **restructured**. Unemployment skyrocketed. The country almost defaulted on its sovereign obligations to foreign **creditors**. In the end, the government asked the International Monetary **Fund** for **assistance** and the IMF offered a $58.4 billion dollar bailout, on terms that have been hotly disputed ever since. Such were the effects of the Asian **Economic** Crisis on Korea in 1997. This paper, **conversely**, will explore the long-term, short-term, international and **domestic** causes of the 1997 Asian **Economic** Crisis as it related to Korea.

In the mid-1990s, three **factors** began to adversely **affect** the Asian tiger **economies**' ability to raise foreign capital. First, as the United States **recovered** from an early '90s recession, it raised interest rates from about 3% to almost 6%, therefore making it a relatively more attractive destination for international capital. Second, the results of China's **economic** reforms of the

1980s really began to take hold during this time, so that it became a more preferred destination for international, profit-**seeking** capital. Third, Japan's ability to import Asia's **exports** was **restrained** when it entered a recession. This situation in Asia generally was **uniquely** mirrored in Korea. In particular, in 1996, the rate of growth of Korean **exports** slowed from 31% to 15%, GNP growth **declined** from 14.6% to 7.1%, and foreign debt increased from $78 billion to $157 billion.

Debt to Equity Levels

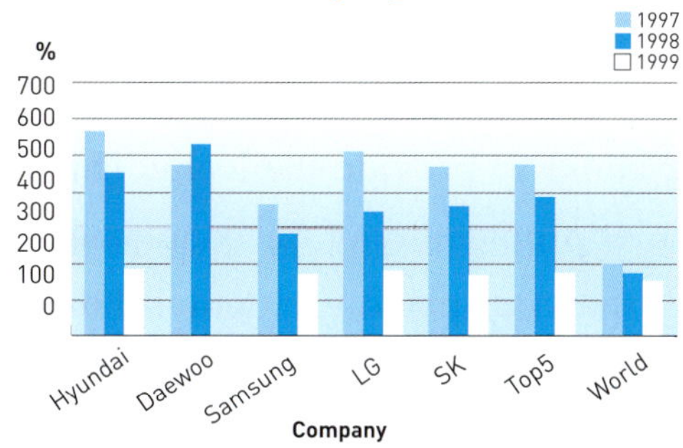

1.______________________________
____
____

Korea had followed a system of state-led development. Private companies were set up to lead in **areas** that were favored by the government, usually **construction** or **exports**. The government then used banks to provide them with capital and gave them **implicit** loan **guarantees**. This **access** to easy, **guaranteed credit** led to the chaebol, too-big-to-fail system with extremely close connections between business and government. In the end, these huge conglomerates built up huge debts which were from two to four times the international average.

2.____
____ While 13 Korean firms were listed in the Fortune 500 in 1997, the top Korean bank was ranked 186th in the Banker's List. Bankers' risk-assessment was underdeveloped. Because of complicated **regulations**, banks, which generally borrowed short-term internationally to lend over the long-term **domestically**, were very vulnerable to **corporate** failure and foreign exchange adjustments. 3.__________________
____

Korea's first premonition of disaster **occurred** in January, 1997, when

Hanbo Steel declared bankruptcy with a debt burden of 22 times its equity. This had several nasty effects. First, it showed the overextended nature of Korean banks, when it was discovered that Korea First Bank had lent an amount almost equal to its value to one risky borrower. Second, it **highlighted** the ties, both **legal** and **illegal**, between big business and government in directing banks to provide the loans. Thirdly, it **exposed** the excess **capacity** and lack of profitability of the conglomerates that were racing to out-**expand** rather than out-profit each other. **Finally**, according to Kim Kihwan, Chair of the Seoul **Finance** Forum, it signaled the government's willingness to now let large companies fail. In the end, the government had to provide $7 billion to the banking system to prevent the **collapse** of several large banks. Hanbo's bankruptcy was followed by that of Samni, another steel maker, two affiliates of the Jinro group, the Dainong retail chain, the Ssangyong business group, and Kia motors, all by July. Something was seriously wrong at Korea Inc.

4.____ ____ According to Thai economist, Narisa Laplamwanit, Thailand experienced large foreign capital inflows throughout the early 1990s. When Thai **exports** began to slow in 1996, non-performing loans at the banks began to increase. Foreigners began to withdraw from the market so that capital became harder to find, the **economy** slowed further, and the exchange rate came under pressure. Thailand had been following an exchange rate fixed at about 25 baht to the U.S. dollar, and attempted to defend it, but the government's American dollar reserves went from $30 billion to $2 billion by June. International speculators had by this time sensed weakness, so that in May they launched a massive speculative attack. In July, the government surrendered and moved to a **flexible** exchange rate system. The value of the baht plummeted to 48.8 baht per dollar. 5. ____

____

This turbulence led foreign banks to refuse to roll over their short-term loans to Asian debtors, including Korea's heavily indebted banks. These loans had to be repaid in dollars, which became more and more difficult, as the value of the won **collapsed**. The Korean government tried to pass a financial reform package to deal with the situation, but failed. Foreign currency reserves were used up trying to support the exchange rate and the banks. Insolvency loomed. On November 21, 1997, the Korean government requested **assistance** from the International Monetary **Fund**.

Subsequent events belong to another essay. 1998 was not an easy year for Korea, but 1999 saw improvement. The Korean government **instituted policies** intended to prevent anything like this from ever happening again. By 2000, the Korean **economy**, though changed by the crisis, had almost completely **recovered**. All the loans from the IMF were soon repaid.

Reading Strategy | Supporting Main Ideas

When trying to support a **thesis**, **authors** need to **focus** on the most important **factors** to prove their **thesis** and **highlight** its importance. **As previously** mentioned, they then need to support these **factors** with **specific** supporting information such as statistics, **expert** opinion, personal experience, personal opinion, related ideas and details. The general rule to keep in mind is: the more *specific and relevant the information, the better it will support the point you are trying to make.*

Main Idea

- In the mid-1990s, three **factors** began to adversely **affect** the tiger **economies**' ability to raise foreign capital.

Supporting Information

- (**statistic**) The United States raised interest rates from about 3% to almost 6%, therefore making it a relatively more attractive destination for international capital.
- (detail)The results of China's **economic** reforms of the 1980s really began to take hold during this time, so that it began to become a more preferred destination for international, profit-**seeking** capital.
- (detail) Japan's ability to import Asia's **exports** was **restrained** when it entered a recession.

Task 7-3

1. Look back at the reading and find **specific** supporting details for the main ideas listed below.

Main Idea

- **Banks in Korea were underdeveloped and weak.**

Supporting Information

a)____

b)____
c)____
d)____

Main Idea

Korea's first premonition of disaster **occurred** in January, 1997, when Hanbo Steel declared bankruptcy.

Supporting Information

a)____
b)____
c)____
d)____
e)____

2. Among the different types of **specific** supporting details, which appear most effective? Which do you think are least effective? Why?
3. In which order of importance are the supporting details listed? In other words, does the most important supporting detail come first, in the middle, or last? Why do you think this is so?

Comprehension Questions

Task 7-4

1. What is the main idea of this article?
2. "The country almost defaulted on its sovereign obligations to foreign **creditors**." Put this **quote** into your own words.
3. How much money did the International Monetary Fund agree to lend Korea?
4. How were the factors that began to adversely affect the Asian tiger economies reflected in the Korean economy?

5. What special, "made-in-Korea" **factors** helped bring the general Asian **economic** crisis of 1997 to Korea?
6. What special problems did Korean banks have that made them vulnerable?
7. a) What was the "premonition of disaster" that the **author** mentioned?
   b) What problems did this event **highlight**?
8. Explain the progression of events that led to the collapse of the Thai baht by filling in the cause and effect chain. The first and last events have been done for you.

9. Fill in the cause and effect chain that led from the devaluation of the Thai baht to the Korean government requesting help from the International Monetary **Fund**.

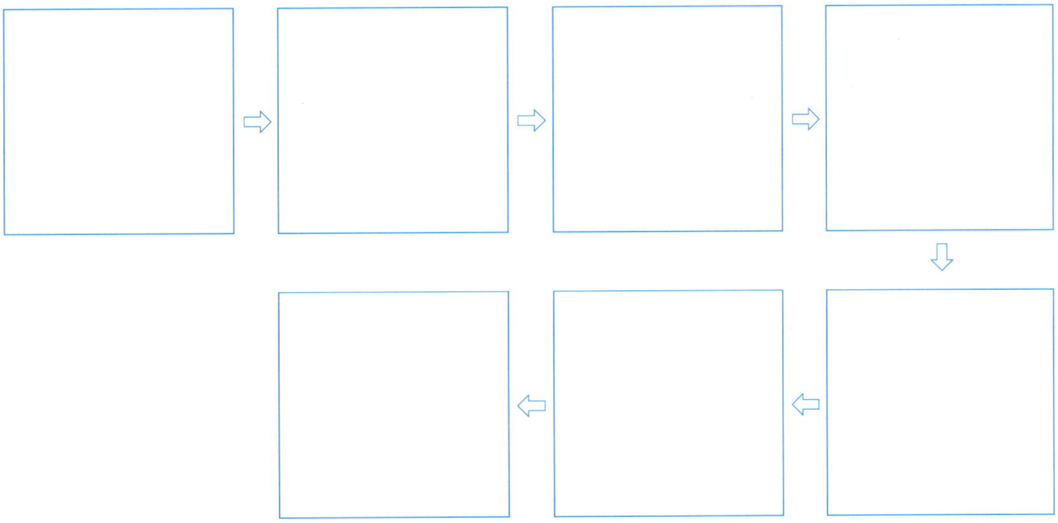

Reaction Questions

Task 7-5

Discuss the following questions with a **partner**.

1. What **unique** skills and abilities do you believe Korea has to sell to the world?
2. Do you believe that the current **economic** system in Korea and the world is the best that could possibly be? If not, how could it be improved?
3. The Asian **Economic** Crisis **created** a great deal of **debate** about a) the International Monetary **Fund**, b) large, international banks, c) **currency** traders, and d) Korean conglomerates. With a **partner**, discuss, in turn, your opinions of each of the above **entities**.
4. Write one more question that you would like to ask your **partner** about the **topic**.

   ▶ ____

5. Write about 150 words on one of the **topics** above. Include five words from the **Academic** Word List, **highlighted** in bold.

Writing Strategy | Article Review

An article review summarizes and gives one's opinion about another piece of writing. There are many different ways to do this, but we will show you a simple yet highly effective, four-**paragraph method**.

The first **paragraph** is an introductory **paragraph**. For different **methods** of writing introductory **paragraphs**, review the **relevant section** of **chapter** six.

The second **paragraph** is a **summary** of the article being reviewed. For **summary methods**, review the **relevant section** of **chapter** five.

The third **paragraph** gives the **author**'s opinion of the article. See below for tips on how to write a persuasive **paragraph**.

The **concluding paragraph** can be written using one of the **methods** from **chapter** six. Another **method** for writing **concluding paragraphs**, useful especially when dealing with opinion, is to introduce an opinion that opposes your own, and then refute it. There is an example of that in the example article below.

Example Article Review

Non-**Rational Economics** and the Asian **Financial** Crisis

It seems that one of the more unattractive **features** of modern-day capitalism is its vulnerability to crisis. From the various crises of the nineteenth century to the Great **Depression** of the 1930s, to the American banking disaster of 2008, recessions are endemic and unpleasant. In "Korea and the Asian **Economic** Crisis of 1997," Robert Jeens has tried to outline the causes of one of these downturns. Unfortunately, the mainstream view which he takes fails to **adequately** explain the **phenomenon** he **seeks** to describe.

Jeens looks at the crisis from both international and **domestic perspectives**. Internationally, he **analyzes** the reasons for the flight of international capital from the East Asian **region**. He sees long-term **trends** which culminated in a banking and foreign exchange meltdown in Thailand. This then spread to countries throughout the **region**, including Korea. Korea was **uniquely** vulnerable, again, because of structural weaknesses endemic to its **economy**. These weaknesses had long-term causes due to imbalances that had built up, and to which its government **reacted** poorly. Thus came the flight of foreign capital, the c**ollapse** of the won, the near-bankruptcy of the country, and the resort to the International Monetary **Fund**.

This narrow view fails to take into account the views of non-**rational economics** and the "herd" behavior of international **currency** speculators. The main reason for the Asian **Financial** Crisis was not structural weaknesses in the Korean or other Asian **economies**. A 1997 IMF report **initially** reported that Korea would escape the crisis. **Similarly**, the Managing Director of the IMF in Singapore declared that he did not understand why the crisis was spreading from Thailand to the larger **region**. Frederic Mishkin **found** that a relatively small risk was magnified by asymmetric information which led to a panicked **reaction** with a massive, "herd-like" capital outflow on the **behalf** of foreign capital. This was the key event that brought everything else. Chandra Hardy, who is a retired **economist** at the Word Bank, wrote that, "**currency** speculators roamed the waters of East Asia like sharks smelling blood." The problem was that the speculators were more powerful (had more money) than most national governments, so once they began to speculate against a national **currency**, the governments lost.

Jeens' article **highlights** the differences between **rational** and non-**rational economics**. **Rational economics** looks at structural, real-world reasons for **economic** behavior, while non-**rational economics** uses **insights** gained from **psychology** to **analyze** the idiosyncrasies of human behavior which can have huge **impacts** upon the real-world **economy**. Of course, that is not to **deny** that there were some structural weaknesses that were **exposed** by the crisis. They were there. However, they in themselves did not cause the crisis, and over time they may have been **resolved** by other means.

Task 7-6

Structural **Analysis** of "Non-**Rational Economics** and the Asian **Financial** Crisis"

1. Review the types of introductory paragraph **found** on page 123 and 124. Which is this?
2. What is the **thesis** statement of the essay?
3. What other essential information is included in the introductory **paragraph**?
4. What is the main idea of the second **paragraph**?
5. How does the **author** support this main idea?
6. What type of **paragraph** is the second **paragraph**?
7. What is the main idea of the third **paragraph**?
8. How does the **author** support this main idea?
9. What type of paragraph is the third paragraph?
10. What **techniques** does the **author** use in the **concluding paragraph**?

Persuasive Paragraph

In a persuasive **paragraph**, the **author** tries to persuade her audience to do something or agree with the **author** in some way. Persuasion is probably the most common form of **academic** writing; for example, "Which Korean city, province or ecoregion would you like to live in?" or, "Who was your best teacher ever?" are both examples of persuasive writing. In an article review, you simply try to persuade someone of your view of an article.

Task 7-7

Fill in the **relevant** information from the third paragraph of the article, "Non-**Rational** Economics and the Asian **Financial** Crisis.

Persuasive **Paragraph** Organization
Topic Sentence – Opinion stated directly.
Reason A **Specific** Supporting Information
Reason B **Specific** Supporting Information
Reason C **Specific** Supporting Information
Concluding Sentence

Some Problems with **Evidence** and **Logic**

Even when using facts, writers of argument must be especially careful to avoid mistakes of **evidence** and **logic**. Here are five of the most common **errors**.

- False *Conclusion*: The **conclusion** is not based on proper **evidence**.
  I like 2%. You like 2%. Therefore, 2% is the most popular drink in Korea.

- *Misplaced Causes and Effects*: Just because one thing takes place before another doesn't mean it causes it; **similarly**, just because one thing follows another does not mean it is an effect of it.

  Your teacher came to Korea in 1996. **Consequently**, Korea suffered from the IMF monetary crisis in 1997.

- *Bad **Evidence***: **Evidence** is used that comes from an outdated, incompetent or **biased source**.

  According to Yonsei professor Robert Jeens, Yonsei University is the best university in the world.

- *Ad Hominem*: This is an attack on a person's character rather than the strength oftheir argument.

  Ex-President Bill Clinton's relationship with Monica Lewinsky has made him **obviously** unable to **comment** on Korea's **economy**.

- *Straw Man*: The opponent's argument is oversimplified, and the writer then attacks the oversimplified argument.

  When you say that handguns should be banned, you are attacking all gun owners.

Task 7-8

Study the following statements. What problems does each have?

1. The protestors are just a bunch of angry, **professional** thugs, so we shouldn't listen to anything they say.

   Problem: ________________________________

2. People who support free trade with the U.S.A. don't care about Korean farmers.

   Problem: ________________________________

3. Soccer became a very popular sport because of the large crowds that came to see the games.

Problem: ________________________________

4. Australia is the best place to live in the world, says the Australian **Prime** Minister.

Problem: ________________________________

5. English has the most words of any language. Therefore, English is the best language on earth.

Problem: ________________________________

6. I ate the fish and now I am sick. The fish must have made me sick.

Problem: ________________________________

7. Both George W. Bush and Barrack Obama have admitted to using cocaine when they were young. How can we believe anything they say?

Problem: ________________________________

8. If we ban heaters, we can prevent fires in the winter.

Problem: ________________________________

9. You wear glasses? **Obviously**, you can not properly **identify** this man.

Problem: ________________________________

10. The suspect played video games 10 hours a day. They caused his violent behavior.

Problem: ________________________________

Sentence Building: **Adjective Clauses**

Restrictive (Essential) Adjective **Clauses**

• Private firms were set up to lead in **areas** that were favored by the government.

In this example, the adjective **clause** is essential to the sentence. If you delete the adjective clause, the sentence is nonsensical.

"[F]avored by the government" tells us which **areas**.

• We can use *that*.

• We can leave out *that/who/which* when the adjective clause is the object of the sentence.

• We don't use commas.

Non**restrictive** (Extra Information) Adjective **Clauses**

• Banks, which generally borrowed short-term internationally to lend over the long-term **domestically**, were very vulnerable to **corporate** failure and foreign exchange **adjustments**.

In this example, the adjective **clause** does not give us essential information. If we **remove** the adjective **clause**, the sentence will keep the most important meaning.

• We cannot use *that*; we must use *who* or *which*.

• We cannot leave out *who* or *which*.

• We use commas with non-**restrictive** relative **clauses**.

Task 7-9

Unscramble the relative clauses in the sentences and check your answers in the article.

1. In the end, these huge conglomerates built up huge debts which/average/the international/times/ two to four/from/were .

   ⊙ ______________________________

2. These loans had to be repaid in dollars, which/difficult/more/more/and/became/, as the value of the won rapidly **declined**.

⊙ ____________________

3. The mainstream view/he/takes/which/fails to **adequately** explain the **phenomenon** he **seeks** to describe.

⊙ ____________________

4. Chandra Hardy,/a retired **economist**/is/at the Word Bank/who/,wrote that, "**currency** speculators roamed the waters of East Asia like sharks smelling blood."

⊙ ____________________

Task 7-10

Connect the sentences by making relative **clauses**. You will have to add and delete words.

1. The Asian **Financial** Crisis had a huge **impact** upon Korea. The **impact** lingered for years

⊙ ____________________

2. Many people lost their **jobs**. They had had these **jobs** for many years.

⊙ ____________________

3. The number of homeless people swelled. The homeless people gathered at places like Seoul Station.

⊙ ____________________

4. Some people were heavily in debt. They **committed** suicide.

⊙ ____________________

5. Others sold gold jewelry. The jewelry had been given to them as a marriage present.

⊙ ____________________

6. Some cashed in their American dollars. They had collected the dollars as insurance against hard times.

▶ ______________________________

7. Companies were **restructured**. These companies had received bail-out money.

▶ ______________________________

8. The accounts of the large Korean conglomerates were made more transparent. The reckless **expansion** of the large Korean conglomerates was seen as partly to blame for the crisis.

▶ ______________________________

9. The I.M.F. demanded that the Korean **economy** become more open to imports. Large I.M.F. donors included Japan and America.

▶ ______________________________

10. In the end, the Korean government paid back all the I.M.F. loans. The Korean government did not want to continue under I.M.F. supervision.

▶ ______________________________

Academic Vocabulary: Verbs 2

Task 7-11

You must put the word that follows the sentence into its correct verb form and use it to fill in the blank in the sentence. Check these sentences with the original sentences from the **text** to see how different word forms are used.

1. There is a vast system of private educational **institutes** that __________ the public system. (**parallel**) (104)
2. In order to really improve your English you must __________________ to **communicate** in English. (**resolve**) (121)

3. This crisis __________ as international capital **disinvested** in not only Thailand, but also Indonesia. (**regional**) (126)
4. The government asked the International Monetary **Fund** __________ it. (**assistance**) (126)
5. The government __________ bank loans for some favored companies. (**guarantees**) (127)
6. The chaebol __________ easy, **guaranteed credit**. (**access**) (127)
7. Large Korean conglomerates recklessly __________, which was seen as partly to blame for the crisis. (**expansion**) (128)
8. Thailand __________ fewer goods in 1996. (**exports**) (128)
9. Foreign capital __________ to a relatively small risk with a massive, "herd-like" capital outflow. (**reaction**) (135)
10. The idiosyncrasies of human behavior hugely __________ the real-world **economy**. (**impacts**) (136)

Academic Writing Assignment: Article Review

1. Choose an article to review. You may review one of the reading passages in this book, or another article, with the permission of your teacher. Use at least five words from the **Academic** Word List that have appeared in the book so far. Type the words in bold so that your teacher can easily identify them.

The Writing Process

2. Review **chapter** 5 and **summarize** your article according to the **method** suggested there.
3. Plan a persuasive **paragraph** in which you give your opinion of the article. To get ideas, you may want to freewrite, brainstorm, or cluster. Keep the best ideas, and try to develop them. The **topic** sentence must directly state your opinion.

Remember to support your opinion with **specific** details which are filled with relevant facts. Avoid problems of **evidence** and **logic**. Finish with a **concluding** sentence that leaves the reader with a strong impression.

4. Write an introductory **paragraph** with a **thesis** statement. **Cite** the **author** and title of the article.
5. Write a **concluding paragraph** which leaves a strong impression with the reader.
6. Make sure that there are **transition** sentences between some of the **paragraphs**.
7. Check the essay against the essay checklist below. Correct the mistakes, rewrite the essay, and hand it in to your teacher. It should be about 2 pages long, 12-point type, double-spaced.

Article Review Structure
Introductory Paragraph • Cite the author and title of the article. • Include your thesis statement.
Summary Paragraph • Summarize the article in one paragraph, utilizing the techniques from Chapter 5.
Persuasive Paragraph • The topic sentence should directly state your opinion of the article. • Support your opinion with relevant evidence.
Concluding Paragraph • Leave your reader with a strong impression.

Article Review Checklist

Form
- Are there four **paragraphs**?
- Is the essay about two pages, double-spaced, with 12-point type?

Organization
- Does the introductory **paragraph cite** the author and title of the article?
- Does the introductory **paragraph** include a **thesis** statement?
- Is there at least one **transition** sentence between **paragraphs**?
- Does the **concluding paragraph** leave the reader with a lasting impression?

Content
- Do the title and introductory paragraph arouse interest?
- Is the essay language direct and **clear**?
- Does the essay use **appropriate** vocabulary?
- Does the essay use a variety of sentence **structures** to make it more interesting?
- Does the **topic** sentence of the **summary paragraph** contain the main idea of the **summarized** article?
- Does the **summary paragraph** contain the most important details of the **summarized** article?
- Does the **topic** sentence of the persuasive **paragraph** directly state the writer's opinion?
- Is the **specific** supporting information in the persuasive **paragraph** strong and **relevant**?
- Are there at least five words from the **Academic** Word List in bold?

Grammar and Mechanics
- Does the writer avoid mistakes of spelling, capitalization and punctuation?
- Are there any mistakes of singular or plural?
- Does the writer avoid sentence fragments?
- Does the writer use correct verb **tenses**?
- Are conjunctions used correctly?
- Do the nouns, pronouns and verbs agree with each other?
- Are prepositions used correctly?
- Are noun, verb, adjective and adverb forms used correctly?
- Are articles used correctly?

Chapter

08 Korean History

Korean History Quiz

Partner A, stay here.

Partner B, go to page 156.

Read the questions below to your **partner**. The correct answer is underlined. Who received the highest score?

---

1. What was the name of the first newspaper to be **published** in Korean and English,?

   a) Chosun Daily b) Capital Gazette c) <u>The Independent</u>

2. What occasion did the leaders of the Gapsin Coup use to begin their plot?

   a) the King's birthday b) <u>the opening of the new Postal **Administration**</u>

   c) the beheading of the traitor Lee Bum Suk

3. What year did Korea become independent from Japan?

   a) 1910 b) <u>1945</u> c) 1950

4. What was the name of the American General put in charge of the **occupational** government in Korea in 1945?

   a) Harry Truman b) Douglas MacArthur c) <u>John Hodge</u>

5. When was Subway Line Number 1 completed from Seoul Station to Cheongnyangni?

   a) 1972 b) <u>1974</u> c) 1976

Focus Question

Task 8-1

The writing passage below is about a famous Korean-American named Seo Jae-pil, or Philip Jaisohn. What do you know about him? Share your information with a **partner**.

Task 8-2 Vocabulary

Match the words on the left with their **definitions** on the right.

1. _____ an aristocrat
2. _____ a cabinet
3. _____ corruption
4. _____ a coup
5. _____ delegation
6. _____ a legation
7. _____ a nationalist
8. _____ a plotter

a) a member of the class who hold high social rank
b) a person who wants political independence for their country
c) a group of people sent from their country to represent it
d) an attempt to take over the government of a country by force
e) a member of a group that is attempting to do something secret and **illegal** or harmful
f) an office in which representatives from another country work, with less importance than an embassy
g) a group of people who control the different departments of a government
h) immoral or **illegal** behavior by people in power

Reading Strategy | Highlighting and Annotating Text

Task 8-3 **Highlighting** and annotating **text** is useful for two reasons. First, it will help you to understand the **text**. Second, it will **aid** you when you need to study the information for a test. Instead of re-reading the entire **text**, all you need to do is go over the information that you have **highlighted** and annotated.

As you read, **highlight topic** sentences, as they contain the most important information. Next, **highlight** supporting details and key words. **Finally**, you can make comments upon your notes in the **margins**. Do you have any questions about the information that has been presented? Is there anything that you would wish to study further? Practice on the reading passage below and turn to page 152 to compare that answer with yours.

The First Modern Korean?

Seo Jae-pil (Philip Jaisohn) was a Korean aristocrat, student at a Japanese **military academy**, **revolutionary**, American-trained doctor, newspaperman, nationalist, and spokesman for the American **occupation** forces in Seoul. He played very active roles in some of the **crucial** events of late nineteenth and early twentieth century Korea that often put him in **conflict** with whatever **authority** was in power in Seoul. His long life reads like an adventure novel; it was almost too good to be true. His ideas were prescient: while unsuccessful at the time, modern Korea has actually embraced most of the values that he **advocated**.

Mr. Seo was born an aristocrat in Jeolla Province in 1864. He lived in the **style** and received an education **appropriate** to members of this privileged class. He grew up in Seoul, where he became an observer of politics from

a very young age. He later claimed that he became **aware** of the wealth and social differences between him and most other children. In 1883, he led a 12-strong Korean student delegation to the Japanese **military academy**. He imbibed the reformist and nation-strengthening sentiments current in Japan at the time while there. He also fell under the influence of Kim Ok-kyun, probably the most prominent **advocate** of reform in Korea at the time.

Upon his return to Korea in 1884, the twenty-year-old **found** his plans for the reform of his country frustrated. The court was under the influence of the conservative family of Queen Min, who was allied with the influential and conservative Chinese envoy to Korea, Yuan Sei-kai.

The **response** of Seo and other **similarly**-minded young men such as the above-mentioned Kim Ok-gyun, was the Gapsin Coup. On December 4, 1884, the plotters set fire to a palace building, using this as a pretense to move the king and his family to Kyongu Palace, where they could be more easily controlled. With the king under the guard of Seo, 12 students, and 125 soldiers from the Japanese legation, the reformers killed 6 prominent conservative politicians and **issued** a 14-point reform edict calling, among other things, for the abolition of the aristocracy and independence from China. The coup plotters, however, had neither popular nor political support and their effort was crushed after 3 days, when 1500 Chinese troops, under Yuan Shi-Kai, "rescued" the King and Queen. Eight of the plotters managed to escape Korea, while the rest were killed. The reform movement in Korea was severely compromised. Mr. Seo recalls that he and three others left Seoul together on December 8 "in the midst of rocks and tiles thrown at us along the streets of

Seoul." They walked to Incheon and set sail for Japan.

After a difficult winter in Japan, Seo decided to try his luck in San Francisco. He held several menial **jobs** and learned English at night school at the YMCA. **Finally**, he met a wealthy sponsor who brought him to Pennsylvania, where he attended preparatory school (the first Korean to do so) for 3 years. Philip Jaisohn then spent the next 9 years working and studying at George Washington University, where he became the first Korean to earn a **medical** degree in the United States. During this time, he also became the first Korean to become an American citizen (in 1890), and he married Muriel Armstrong in 1894, with whom he later had two daughters.

Following political changes in Korea that included the Sino-Japanese war of 1895, the murder of Queen Min and the ascendance of a Japanese-**dominated**, reform cabinet, Seo Jae Pil was invited back to Korea in 1895. He **declined** an invitation of a cabinet post but returned in 1896 with the intention of **advocating** modernization and democracy. He bought a printing press in Japan and **established** the first newspaper **published** in both English and Korean, entitled "The Independent" in April, 1896. **Despite** the king's flight to the Russian legation, the following rise of the conservative faction at court, and the murder or exile of the pro-Japan cabinet members, Seo was allowed to continue his activities with the newspaper. The newspaper generally supported **concepts** such as democracy, public hygiene, public education and national independence.

Later in 1896, Seo **established** the Independence Club, a group of reform-minded politicians and citizens who combined to **advocate** modernization. The group criticized government **policies**, often quite harshly, and after a time came under censure. At the same time, as a **symbol** of national pride, Seo **designed** and raised money for the Independence Gate to be erected on the site where, for centuries, Korean kings used to meet Chinese envoys dispatched to Seoul. As criticisms of the government in his newspaper and at his club became harsher, however, Seo came under increasing pressure from that same government. Officials who were criticized for corruption and conservatism became increasingly hostile to Seo and his activities. In 1898, Seo, charged with **advocating** republicanism, was forced to leave Korea; also, the newspaper and club were destroyed and disbanded.

Upon his return to the United States, Philip Jaisohn **conducted medical research** at the University of Pennsylvania. At the same time, he remained **involved** in Korean expatriate politics so that, upon hearing news of the March First Movement in 1919, he **convened** the First Korean Congress in Philadelphia. From then on, he **devoted** himself to Korean independence from Japan, meeting with other prominent Korean nationalists, fundraising and engaging in letter-writing campaigns, vainly looking for help and **intervention**, particularly from his adopted country. Unfortunately, his activities left him bankrupt by 1924, so that he had to return to medicine and printing to make a living. **Finally**, he **aided** his adopted country during World War Two as an army doctor.

Seo was again invited back to his original homeland after Korea's **liberation** from Japan in 1945. Although he had many supporters who urged him to **assume** political leadership, he **declined** and returned as a spokesperson for the American **Occupational** government in 1947. He gave his returning address at Seoul Stadium to 50,000 cheering people. Later, he gave several radio broadcasts **advocating themes** he had always held dear: democracy, education, modernization. His ailing health necessitated his return to America in 1948.

Broken by old age and war in his country, Philip Jaisohn died in 1951. He had lived quite a life, from aristocrat to reformer, **revolutionary** to exile, doctor, newspaperman, and elder statesman. He was distraught by the division of his country and the lack of progress in the causes he had always supported. However, his **advocacy** of these causes presaged an age to come, when the ideas he had always espoused **finally** prevailed.

Highlighting and Annotating Text

The First Modern Korean?

very active

failure

Seo Jae-pil (Philip Jaisohn) was a Korean aristocrat, student at a Japanese **military academy, revolutionary**, American-trained **medical** doctor, newspaperman, nationalist, and, spokesman for the American **occupation** forces in Seoul. He played very active **roles** in some of the **crucial** events of late nineteenth and early twentieth century Korea that often put him in **conflict** with whatever **authority** was in power in Seoul. His long life reads like an adventure novel; it was almost too good to be true. His ideas were prescient: while unsuccessful at the time, modern Korea has actually embraced most of the values that he **advocated**.

Thesis statement

priveleged

Mr. Seo was born an aristocrat in Jeolla Province in 1864. He lived in the **style** and received an education **appropriate** to members of this privileged class. He grew up in Seoul, where he became an observer of politics from

a very young age. He later claimed that he became aware of the wealth and social differences between him and most other children. In 1883, he led a 12-strong Korean student delegation to the Japanese **military academy**. He imbibed the reformist and nation-strengthening sentiments current in Japan at the time while there. He also fell under the influence of Kim Ok-kyun, probably the most prominent **advocate** of reform in Korea at the time.

Connection to Gapsin Coup?

Upon his return to Korea in 1884, the twenty-year-old **found** his plans for the reform of his country frustrated. The court was under the influence of the conservative family of Queen Min, who was allied with the influential and conservative Chinese envoy to Korea, Yuan Sei-kai.

The **response** of Seo and other **similarly**-minded young men such as the above-mentioned Kim Ok-gyun, was the Gapsin Coup. On December 4, 1884, the plotters set fire to a palace building, using this as a pretense to move the king and his family to Kyongu Palace, where they could be more easily controlled. With the king under the guard of Seo, 12 students, and 125 soldiers from the Japanese legation, the reformers killed 6 prominent conservative politicians and **issued** a 14-point reform edict calling, among other things, for the abolition of the aristocracy and independence from China. The coup plotters, however, had neither popular nor political support and their effort was crushed after 3 days, when 1500 Chinese troops, under Yuan Sei-Kai, "rescued" the King and Queen.

failure

in charge

Reading Strategy | Inference

Inference consists of reasoning from incomplete pieces of information to find someone's **implied** opinion.

Task 8-4

Answer the questions below to practice **inferring**.

1. Does the **author** believe that the end result of the Gapsin Coup was **positive** or **negative**? Why?
2. What is the **author**'s opinion of Philip Jaisohn's activities in America between 1919 and 1924? How do you know this?
3. What **indicated** that Seo Jae-pil was still a popular figure in 1948?

Comprehension Questions

Task 8-5

1. What is the main idea of the article?

   a) Seo Jae Pil's life was so exciting that it would make a good adventure novel.
   b) Seo Jae Pil was the first Korean to do many things in America.
   c) Seo Jae Pil opposed first the Korean government and then the Japanese **occupation**.
   d) Most of Seo Jae Pil's ideas for the modernization of Korea were realized, but only after his death.

2. List at least three pieces of information that support the main idea above.
3. Seo Jae Pil was the first Korean to do many things. List them.
4. Detail Philip Jaisohn's life in America from 1885 to 1895 on this timeline.

1885	1886	1887	1888	1889	1890	1891	1892	1893	1894	1895

5. What led Seo Jae-pil to be invited back to Korea in 1895?
6. Why was he forced to leave Korea in 1898?
7. What led Philip Jaisohn to **convene** the First Korean **Conference** in 1919?
8. What setback did Philip Jaisohn suffer in 1924? What caused this and what was the effect of this?
9. Seo Jae Pil **declined** political leadership in Korea twice. When was this?
10. Choose the correct answer.

    Philip Jaisohn was an army doctor in: a) Korea.
    b) Japan
    c) the U.S.A.
11. How old was Philip Jaisohn when he died?

Korean History Quiz

Partner B, stay here.

Partner A, go to page 146.

Read the questions below to your **partner**. The correct answer is underlined. Who received the highest score?

1. Who was Yuan Shi Kai?

a) <u>Chinese Ambassador to Korea, 1884</u>

b) Chinese Ambassador to Korea, 1895 c) Chinese Ambassador to Korea, 1951

2. To where did King Kojong flee in 1896?

a) <u>The Russian Legation</u> b) Ganghwa Island c) The South Han Fortress

3. What major landmark was built in Seoul in 1897?

a) Namdaemun Market b) Seoul Station c) <u>Independence Gate</u>

4. Who was the first president of the Republic of Korea?

a) <u>Syngman Rhee</u> b) Chung Hee Park c) Il Sung Kim

5. What year did Korea host the Olympics?

a) 1984 b) 1986 <u>c) 1988</u>

Reaction Questions

Task 8-6

Discuss the following questions with a **partner**.

1. Do you think the monarchy, and King Kojong in particular, had a **positive** or **negative impact** on Korean history?
2. What is your opinion of the Japanese colonial government in Korean history? Why?

3. What do you think is the most glorious **period** of Korean history?

4. Write one more question you would like to ask your **partner**.

▶ ____

5. Write 100 to 150 words on any of the **topics** above. Include five words from the **Academic** Word List, **highlighted** in bold.

Writing Strategy | Narrative Essays

Narratives tell stories. Because there are many types of stories, narratives usually allow the writer more freedom to be creative than other essays. However, a narrative essay can still contain an introductory **paragraph** with a **thesis** statement, a body with supporting **paragraphs**, each with **topic** sentences and **linked** by **transition** sentences, and a **concluding paragraph**.

Narrative essays contain several **unique** characteristics. There is a setting or settings. That is, the story takes place someplace which has some importance to the story. There is a plot, or story. As it is impossible to tell every little detail in the story, the most important or **relevant** parts of the plot are **emphasized** to make it complete and interesting. There are characters, or the people in the story. They are **affected** by or **initiate** the events that take place. This is true of all narratives, whether fiction or non-fiction.

Biography: A Story of a Life

Biography is one type of narrative, so that all the above facts about narrative are true for biography, as well. A person's life story is told. A biography makes arguments about the **significance** of events in a person's life, and the **significance** of a person's life accomplishments. A **theme** for the person's life is chosen, and the events which support that **theme** are **highlighted**. You should think about questions such as the following.

- Why is this person special or interesting?
- What effects did she have on the world or other people?
- What important events **defined** or changed this person's life?
- What important obstacles did he overcome?

When you write a biography, you need to choose a person to write about. Often this is a famous or infamous person, but sometimes biographies written about ordinary people can be quite interesting. The key is to find interesting things to write about rather than just a bunch of boring facts.

You can start your biography with an interesting statement, like any other essay. **Contrast** the two following opening sentences

- "Betty White was born on April 2, 1940."
- "World War Two was raging across Europe, tanks, airplanes and guns were emptying their deadly rounds, thousands were dying, and amidst it all was heard a small cry of life."

The key to using the more interesting opening is that you need to make it **relevant** by leading into a **thesis** statement by the end of the first **paragraph**. This is the **theme** of the essay.

- The sense of duty that her father showed by **volunteering** to fight in Europe was passed on to his daughter so that she too **volunteered** for duties that would help others.

You may, on the other hand, wish to use one of the techniques for introductory paragraphs from chapter 6: a plain introductory paragraph, a funnel introduction, or a problem-solution introduction. The exact **method** you use to introduce the essay is not important. What is important is that your introduction is interesting, and that it contains a **thesis** statement.

Once you have an impressive introductory **paragraph**, continue the body of the essay by examining interesting and **relevant** details. Usually we look at a person's childhood and education, family and **professional** life and any specially **defining** personality characteristics. The exact contents will depend upon the person whose life you are examining.

In the **concluding paragraph**, you can **summarize** the main points of the essay and repeat, in different words, your main claim about the subject of the biography. It's usually best not to introduce new facts about the person or to repeat **specific** examples from the body. Review the different **techniques** that were introduced in chapter 6: a plain conclusion, a triangle **conclusion**, and a **predictive conclusion**. Would you like to use one of those types, or something different?

Sentence Building: **Run-on Sentences and Comma Splices**

Run-on Sentences

The following is an example of a run-on sentence.

His long life reads like an adventure novel it's almost too good to be true.

It is called a run-on sentence because it is actually two sentences (His long life reads like an adventure novel. It's almost too good to be true.) strung together incorrectly

Comma Splices

One way that students sometimes try to correct run-on sentences is by **inserting** a comma between two sentences. This is incorrect, and is known as a comma splice.

His long life reads like an adventure novel, it's almost too good to be true.

Correcting Run-On Sentences and Comma Splices

There are several ways to correct run-on sentences and comma splices.

- **Insert** a semi-colon (;) or colon (:) between the two sentences.

  His long life reads like an adventure novel; it's almost too good to be true.

- Connect the two sentences with a conjunction, either **coordinating**, subordinating, or adverbial, with **appropriate** punctuation as necessary.

  His long life reads like an adventure novel because it's almost too good to be true.

- Separate the sentences

  His long life reads like an adventure novel. It's almost too good to be true.

Task 8-7

Read each of the sentences below. If the sentence is grammatically correct, write *OK* in the space beside it. If it is a run-on sentence or a comma splice, write *RO* or *CS* beside it and correct it using one of the **techniques** above.

1. _____ His ideas were prescient, while unsuccessful at the time, modern Korea has actually embraced most of the values that he **advocated**.

   ____

   ____

2. _____ Mr. Seo was born an aristocrat in Jeolla Province in 1864 he lived in the style and received an education **appropriate** to members of this privileged class.

   ____

   ____

3. _____ The coup plotters, however, had neither popular nor political support their effort was crushed after 3 days.

⊙ ______________________________

____

4. _____ Eight of the plotters managed to escape Korea, while the rest were killed; the reform movement in Korea was severely compromised.

⊙ ______________________________

____

5. _____ During this time, he also became the first Korean to become an American citizen (in 1890), and he married Muriel Armstrong in 1894, with whom he later had two daughters.

⊙ ______________________________

____

6. _____ Seo **declined** an invitation of a cabinet post he returned in 1896 with the intention of **advocating** modernization and democracy.

⊙ ______________________________

____

7. _____ In 1898, Seo, charged with **advocating** republicanism, was forced to leave Korea, the newspaper and club were destroyed and disbanded.

⊙ ______________________________

____

8. _____ At the same time, he remained **involved** in Korean expatriate politics, upon hearing news of the March First Movement, he **convened** the First Korean Congress in Philadelphia.

⊙ ______________________________

____

9. _____ He had many supporters who urged him to **assume** political leadership, he **declined** and returned as a spokesperson for the American **Occupational** government in 1947.

▶ ____

____

10. _____ However, his advocacy of these causes presaged an age to come the ideas he had always espoused finally prevailed.

▶ ____

____

Academic Vocabulary: Adverbs 2

Task 8-8

You must put the word that follows the sentence into its correct adverbial form and use it to fill in the blank in the sentence. Check these sentences with the original sentences from the **text** to see how different word forms are used.

1. He can ____________ diagnose sick students. (**expert**) (109)
2. The government then used banks to provide them with capital and **guaranteed** the loans ____________. (**implicit**) (127)
3. Big business and government were connected both ___________ and ___________. (**legal, illegal**) (128)
4. In July, the Thai government surrendered and allowed the exchange rate to float ____________. (**flexible**) (129)
5. He was ____________ educated for a member of this privileged class. (**appropriate**) (148)

6. The Independence Gate ___________ proclaimed Korea's independence from China. (**symbol**) (151)

7. After 1919, Seo ___________ worked for Korean independence from Japan. (**devoted**) (151)

8. Did the Gapsin coup **impact** ___________ or ___________ upon Korean history? (**positive, negative**) (155)

Academic Writing: Biography

In this **assignment**, you are going to write a biography of a family member. Your family member may be either alive or dead, famous or not. Your essay should be about 2 pages long, in 12-point type, double-spaced. Use at least five words from the **Academic** Word List that have appeared in the book .Type the words in bold so that your teacher can easily identify them.

The Writing Process

1. Gather information: If your family member has passed away, you need to get information from living relatives or **documents** such as letters, newspaper articles or diaries. If your family member is still alive, you can interview him to find the information you need.
2. **Select** the information that you wish to write about.
3. Write a plan for the essay, perhaps in the form of a time line. Order important events in time order, and **briefly** describe them.
4. Write an interesting introductory **paragraph**, with a **thesis** statement.
5. Write the body of the essay. Keep the same order as in your time line, but give more detail so that you can show us how the important events of the person's life relate to your **thesis** statement.
6. Write an effective **concluding paragraph**.
7. Check your essay against the essay checklist below.
8. Correct your mistakes and hand in the **final** product to your teacher.

Biography Checklist

Form
- Do the **paragraphs** use correct **paragraph** form?
- Is the essay about 2 pages long, in 12-point-type, double-spaced?

Organization
- Does the introductory **paragraph** make the reader want to keep reading?
- Does the introductory **paragraph** include a **thesis** statement?
- Does the **concluding paragraph** leave the reader with a lasting impression?
- Do the **paragraphs** have **topic** sentences and **concluding** sentences?
- Are there **transition** sentences?
- Do all the ideas in the essay relate to the **thesis** statement

Content
- Is the essay language direct and **clear**?
- Does the essay use **appropriate** vocabulary?
- Does the essay use a variety of sentence **structures** to make it more interesting?
- Are the events in the essay interesting and **relevant**?
- Has the writer provided an in-depth look at the life of her subject?
- Are there at least five words from the **Academic** Word List in bold?

Grammar and Mechanics
- Does the writer avoid mistakes of spelling, capitalization and punctuation?
- Are there any mistakes of singular or plural?
- Does the writer avoid sentence fragments?
- Does the writer use correct verb **tenses**?
- Are conjunctions used correctly?
- Do the nouns, pronouns and verbs agree with each other?
- Are prepositions used correctly?
- Are noun, verb, adjective and adverb forms used correctly?
- Are articles used correctly?
- Are run-on sentences and comma splices avoided?

Appendix 1:Correction Symbols

Symbol	Meaning	Example
P	punctuation **error**	P She lives in Salem, and works in Boston. CORRECTION: She lives in Salem and works in Boston.
SV	subject-verb agreement	S-V My brother study engineering CORRECTION: My brother studies engineering
ART	article **error**	ART ART I don't have a time to do an homework. CORRECTION: I don't have the time to do homework.
CAP	capitalization **error**	CAP CAP CAP my brother goes to harvard university. CORRECTION: My brother goes to Harvard University.
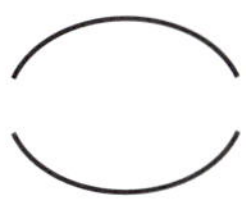	join sentences	John is my best friend. But we are fighting now. CORRECTION: John is my best friend, but we are fighting now.
SING/ PL	singular or plural **error**	PL He likes fast music and fast car. CORRECTION: He likes fast music and fast cars.
SP	spelling mistake	PL He speeks Spanish and French. CORRECTION: He speaks Spanish and French.
VT	wrong verb **tense**	VT He is eating the same thing for lunch every day. CORRECTION: He eats the same thing for lunch every day.

Symbol	Meaning	Example
WF	wrong word form	She is a very nice person and a kindness teacher. (WF)
		CORRECTION: She is a very nice person and a kind teacher.
WW	wrong word	The chair is very convenient. (WW)
		CORRECTION: The chair is very comfortable.
○	word missing	He ate cereal and ○ juice for breakfast.
		CORRECTION: He ate cereal and drank juice for breakfast.
⊘	unnecessary word	She works at the McDonalds now.
		CORRECTION: She works at McDonalds now.
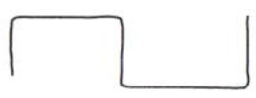	wrong word order	You never are at home when I call.
		CORRECTION: You are never at home when I call.
RO	run-on sentence	We ate dinner then we went out. (RO)
		CORRECTION: We ate dinner, and then we went out.
FRAG	sentence fragment	The movie that we saw last night. (FRAG)
		CORRECTION: I loved the movie that we saw last night.
CS	comma splice	We ate dinner, then we went out. (CS)
		CORRECTION: We ate dinner. Then we went out.

Ⓣ	**transition**	There are many interesting places to visit. Ⓣ There are three temples and two palaces. CORRECTION: There are many interesting places to visit. For example, there are three temples and two palaces.
PREP	preposition **error**	PREP He goes ◯ the office every Saturday. CORRECTION: He goes to the office every Saturday.
CONJ	conjunction error	CONJ So I never like to go there. CORRECTION: Therefore, I never go there.
AWK	awkward phrasing	AWK Bill was the good and seen last night friend. CORRECTION: Bill was the good friend that I saw last night.
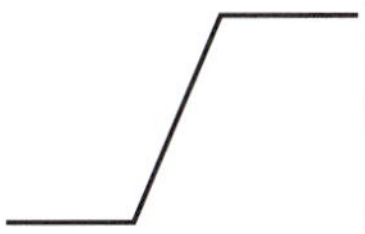	start new paragraph	…and so I went home to bed./When I got up in the morning…. CORRECTION: …and so I went home to bed. When I got up in the morning….

Appendix 2: Mechanics and Grammar

Paragraph Form

Label the following on the paragraph.

b) Title: centered in the middle

c) Left **margin**

d) Right **margin**

e) Indent

f) double spaced

g) 12-point type

h) Date

i) Student name and number

j) **Instructor**'s name

April 5, 2050
Joe Blow 19992155
Ms. Jennifer Mills

Penicillin: The Real Story

Although the story of the accidental discovery of penicillin by Alexander Fleming in 1928 is well-known, it took another 15 years and work by many other **researchers** to **finally** realize the full **potential** of the first modern antibiotic. Fleming understood the **implications** of his discovery but he had trouble **insolating** the antibiotic agent and producing penicillin in quantity. Alexander Fleming did not **solely** develop penicillin. By 1939, Dr. Howard

Florey and Ernest Chain at Oxford University had **insolated** and **concentrated** penicillin; however, they could not produce it in the mass quantities necessary for it to become a widely **available** cure. Unfortunately, they could not make enough. In 1941, Florey and Norman Heatley went to Peoria Lab the US to **seek** help. By 1943, Andrew Moyer, Peoria lab's **expert** on the nutrition of molds, had managed to increase the yield of penicillin 10 times. This made mass production possible, so drug companies began manufacturing penicillin, especially for the treatment of **injured** Allied soldiers.

Capitalization	
1. Capitalize the first word in a sentence.	Where are you going?.
2. Capitalize the pronoun I alone.	At first, I didn't like pizza.
3. Capitalize proper nouns. Proper nouns name **specific** things such as:	
the names of people and their titles,	Professor Park So Young Professor Park So-young
nationalities, languages, religions and **ethnic** groups.	Koreans French Christianity Native Americans
specific places one can find on a map.	England Seoul Elm Street Mount Everest
the names of specific organizations, such as businesses, schools, and clubs.	Hyundai Department Store Konkuk University Jazz Dance Club
the names of days, months, holidays, and special time **periods**.	Monday January new Year's Day The Great **Depression**

4. Don't capitalize common nouns such as: people's titles with no name.	Do you like your math professor?
school subjects generally	biology history
directions generally	north south
the seasons	spring summer
very general names	french fries pasteurize
after commas, semicolons, or colons	First, peel the potatoes.
5. Titles Capitalize the first, last and other important words in a title, but not the small, unimportant words. Usually, verbs, nouns, adjectives, and adverbs are capitalized.	The Lord of the Rings The King and the Clown What's Eating Gilbert Grape? Honey, I Shrunk the Kids

Properly capitalize the two following paragraphs.

the king or the clown?

many people would disagree, but i've always **found** burger king's whoppers to be much more delicious than mcdonalds' big macs. first, the patty: whoppers are thick and char broiled, while big macs have two small, fried patties: score one for the king. next, the bun, which i give an even draw. both have sesame seeds, and while the whopper has two thick buns and the big mac three thin ones, i don't really have a favorite. lastly, let's look at the toppings. the key differences here are that the whopper has tomato, but the big mac has a special sauce and cheese. i really enjoy tomato on a hamburger, but have never liked the special sauce or cheese. in **conclusion**, everybody's tastes are different, but i'll take a whopper anytime.

marshall mcluhan

marshall mcluhan was a 1960s **media** personality and social **commentator** whose **theories** and **quotes** are still widely disseminated and **debated**. born in edmonton, alberta, canada, mcluhan was educated at the university of manitoba and cambridge, where he was awarded his phd in english in 1942. he joined the university of toronto in 1946. although a professor of english, his work **involved analysis** of the importance of **communication** technologies and **media** in history and the contemporary world. by the 1960s, mcluhan was appearing regularly on television, speaking about the transformative power of the electronic **media**. in his book, *the medium is the* ***message***, he explained that technologies like television and radio have not only changed our ability to **communicate**, but also our society. mcluhan **predicted** a "**global** village" where everybody on the planet would be able to **interact** with others intimately though separated by long distances. his **theories** have always been **controversial**, but he was the first person to really understand the importance of the new electronic **media**. marshall mcluhan did not live to see the age of the internet, but had he, we can be sure his **insights** would have been profound.

The Comma (,)	
1. A comma separates a list of three or more things.	He ate coffee, eggs, toast, cereal, and bacon for breakfast. She enjoys reading books, surfing the Internet, and playing golf.
2. A comma separates two sentences when they are combined by a coordinating conjunction such as for, and, nor, but, or, yet, or so.	They were hungry, so they ate a big lunch. I like butterflies, and my wife likes butterflies, too.

3. A comma is used to separate an introductory word or phrase from the main clause.	In conclusion, doctors are advising people to take more vitamins. When I came home, nobody was there.
4. A comma is used to separate out an additional clause at the end of a sentence.	He was fired from his **job**, surprising no one. The **couple** decided upon divorce, their years together now forgotten.
5. A comma is used to separate additional information out from the rest of the sentence. This additional information is a word or group of words that can be taken out of a sentence without greatly **affecting** the meaning.	South Korea, the home of many large conglomerates, has become the eleventh biggest **economy** in the world. My cats, which are spoiled rotten, sleep twenty hours a day. Yonsei University, **located** in Seoul, Korea, is famous for its beautiful campus.
6. A comma is used to separate out dates and quotations.	December 7, 1941, is also known as Pearl Harbor Day. Monday, August 6, 1963 " Billy, " she said, "I love you." "Where did they go?" asked the little boy.
7. A comma is used to separate cities from states and countries	Jill comes from Chicago, Illinois, U.S.A.

Add commas as needed in these sentences.

1. **Despite** all the problems he had as a child William **attained** a good education.
2. I believe the best cities to visit in Asia are Seoul Tokyo Kyoto and Shanghai.
3. The new semester will **commence** on Tuesday September 4 2011.
4. The third step is to add the carrots onions and potatoes.
5. Third add the carrots and potatoes.
6. The **job** interview is for a **contract** at Magna Car Company which is the largest company in this **area**.
7. The **job** interview is for a **contract** at a large company that has more than 1000 employees in this **area**.

8. Kevin's birthday is January 18th which is the same day that Laura and Greg have their birthdays.
9. My **colleague** who lives in Miami has two children. (I have several colleagues.)
10. My **colleague** who lives in Miami has two children. (I have only one colleagues.)
11. This flight is leaving for La Paz which is the first of three stops that the plane will make.
12. No one knows the name of the person who will take over the **commission** in January so there have been many rumors about this.
13. On the right side of the living room an antique radio sits on top of a glass table that also has a flower pot a photo of a baby and a magazine.
14. She asked "What's going on?"
15. So-young likes to read books in the morning but she is often too busy to do so.

The Colon (:)	
1. Use a colon to signal the reader that a second complete sentence explains a closely related **preceding** sentence.	Fish make great pets: if you just feed them once a day, you never have to worry. I love air conditioning: in the summer, it keeps me alive.
2. Use a colon to introduce a list of words, phrases, or clauses that follows a complete sentence.	The Greasy Spoon restaurant had several house specialties: a hot turkey sandwich, a roast pork dinner, and a barbecued chicken wing basket.
3. Use a colon to signal the reader that a name or description follows a complete sentence when you want to put a lot of **emphasis** on that **item**.	The busy thief didn't know who was standing right behind him: a smiling police officer.

Add the **appropriate** punctuation and capitalization to the sentences below.

1. the puppies were cute little bundles of fur
2. hangook tires are known for three characteristics exceptional performance superb **design** and dependable quality
3. diana stared intently at the teacher at the front of the class but olivia who was bored **texted** her friends on her cell phone
4. my parents praised me whenever i received an "A" at school they believed education was very important
5. even though danielle can't swim she **anticipates** going to the beach and watching all the handsome boys in bathing suits
6. the teacher with the most fearsome reputation at my high school had an equally fearsome nickname jaws
7. in my opinion john steinbeck wrote three great books the grapes of wrath of mice and men and east of eden
8. for example the 7:00 pm **lecture** by dr carol danvers at porter hall is entitled **nuclear energy** in canada
9. believing in oneself is absolutely essential for success
10. min hee needs money for her summer vacation so she is working at a part-time **job**
11. after I was finished greedily stealing and eating all my little sister's candy i looked around to see a very unhappy person my mother
12. july 9 1992 was one of the most important days of my life
13. bill evans was one of the greatest jazz pianists of all time his 1959 recording portait in jazz is **considered** a **classic** of improvisation

Add the **appropriate** punctuation and capitalization to the following paragraph.

let someone else drive

seoul in particular and korea in general has a great public **transportation** system the subway is cheap and being extended to more places with more lines all the time seoul station city hall or kangnam the subway will take you wherever you want to go it never gets stuck in traffic so you're always on time watching the beggars peddlers and fellow travelers provides **constant** entertainment the buses are cheap too though perhaps a little less convenient until one figures out the **routes** the new system of bus lanes keeps them flowing along the road quickly and on **schedule** also as korea is a small country with a lot of people the bus and train system out of seoul is extensive and convenient i love taking the train i sit back **relax** let someone else do the driving and arrive on time chances of an accident are so slim as to be **virtually** non-existent cities all around the world could learn a lot from seoul

Sentence Fragments

Decide which groups of words are sentences and which are sentence fragments. Write "S" next to the sentences and FRAG next to the sentence fragments. Correct the sentence fragments to make sentences.

1. _____ Is very hot today.
   ▶ ______________________________
2. _____ My new classmate is from Brazil.
   ▶ ______________________________
3. _____ Help!
   ▶ ______________________________
4. _____ When my children get sick.
   ▶ ______________________________

5. _____ One of the most critical **areas** in the world, East Asia.

⊙ ____

6. _____ Buddhism and Confucianism have influenced Korea's development.

⊙ ____

7. _____ Because Paris is a romantic city.

⊙ ____

8. _____ If the weather is cold.

⊙ ____

9. _____ The Nile is the longest river in the world.

⊙ ____

10. _____ For example, both mathematics and biology.

⊙ ____

Verb Tenses

There is usually a total of 12 English verb **tenses**, depending upon how you describe them. This guide is not meant to be complete, but here is a rough description along with a **couple** of examples of each of the **tenses**. Fill in the blanks using the verb in parentheses. Change the verb **tense** as **indicated**.

Simple Present

Use the simple present to describe an action or state that is usual or repeated. It happens in past, present, and future. e.g) I *am* (be) a teacher. John often _____ (get up) late. We _______ (not like) rain. _____ you _____ (like) milk? He _________ (**attribute**) his success to hard work.

Present Continuous

Use the present continuous to describe an action that is or is not happening now. Speakers sometimes use the present continuous to describe the future. e.g) We *are learning* (learn) English now. Lisa _______ (not pay) attention. _____ you _______ (sleep)? I _______ (meet) my boyfriend after class. Dangerously, the spillway __________ (not **channel**) the water away from the dam.

Present Perfect

We use the present perfect to say that an action, experience or accomplishment happened or did not happen at an **unspecified** time in the past. Speakers also use the present perfect to talk about change that has happened over a **period** of time, to say that an action which we expected has not happened, or to say that several different actions have occurred, but the process is not complete. e.g) My son *has seen* (see) Terminator 15 times. I __________ (not go) to France. ______ Korea ______ (become) a multinational country? You still __________ (not finish) homework. You _______ (write) many compositions in this class. Seoul _________ (**automate**) the subway ticketing system.

Present Perfect Continuous

Use the present perfect continuous to show that something started in the past and continues until now. If you use the present perfect continuous without a **duration** marker, it has more of a meaning of "lately." e.g) Gerard *has been studying* (study) English for 5 years. _____ you ________ (feel) well? Humans __________ (**evolve**) for about 4 million years. Unfortunately, the teacher _________ (not **motivate**) her students this semester.

Simple Past

Use the simple past to describe an action, habit or fact that started and finished or was true at a **specific** time in the past. e.g) I *ate* (eat) soup for lunch today. He _______ (not play) soccer when he was a child. _____ you _____ (like) vegetables when you were a child? Jill __________ (**cease**) crying when she was 10 years old.

Past Continuous

Use the simple past to show that a longer action in the past was interrupted, that two actions were happening at the same time, or, with "always" to show irritation and repetition. e.g) I *was surfing* (surf) the Internet when the doorbell rang. While Sally _______ (work) hard, Billy _______ (spend) her money at the track. What _____ you _____ (do) when you heard about 9-11?

Past Perfect

Use the past perfect to describe an action that **occurred** in the past, before something else. By the time my friend arrived, e.g) I *had cooked* (cook) dinner. Charles ___________ (not finish) eating before he had to go. _____ you _____ (study) English before you moved to Australia? The class __________ (**bond**) well by Christmas.

Past Perfect Continuous

Use the past perfect continuous to **emphasize** the **duration** of an activity that was in progress before something else, or to express that a continuous action was close in time to another activity in the past. e.g) We *had been riding* (ride) our bicycles when it started to rain. Stan __________ (not sleep) well for years, so we were not surprised when he broke down. Where ________________ (live) before you moved here? The **researchers** __________ (conduct) regular tests when they **detected** the radiation leak.

Simple Future

Use the simple future to express future time or willingness. e.g) I *will open* (open) the door. Bill _______ (not dance) with you. _____ you _____ (talk) with your sister tonight? _____ you _________ (**compensate**) your employees for their expenses?

Future Continuous

Use the future continuous to express an action that is going to be in progress at some time in the future. e.g) I *will be working* (work) in my office at 3 pm. Susie __________ (not go) to the party tonight. _____ you be _______ (watch) the hockey game tonight? Sal __________ (demonstrate) the new product at 7pm.

Future Perfect

Use the future perfect **tense** to express an activity that will be completed before another event or time in the future. e.g) By the time my wife *will have finished* (finish) dinner, I _________ (eat) dessert. Susan _________ (not finish) her work before class ends. When _________ (be) in Korea for 5 years? I hope you _______ (**clarify**) that point before the next meeting.

Future Perfect Continuous

Use the future perfect continuous to **emphasize** the **duration** of an activity that will be in progress before another time or event in the future. e.g) She *will have been teaching* (teach) for 30 years when she retires. How long ____ you __________ (drive) before you arrive at Busan? The **environmentalists** ________ (**monitor**) this park for 15 years by 2015.

And, But, Or, and So

Connect the sentences with *and*, *but*, *or*, or *so* to make new sentences. You may have to add or delete some words to make the sentences flow better.

1. I can speak English. I can understand English.
   ▶ ____
2. I can't speak Japanese. I can't speak Vietnamese.
   ▶ ____
3. Would you like soup? Would you like salad? (You may only have one.)
   ▶ ____
4. Franklin Delano Roosevelt, a famous American president, was paralyzed. Franklin Delano Roosevelt, a famous American president, used a wheelchair.
   ▶ ____

5. French used to be the language of international diplomacy. Now English is used more often.

⊙ ____

6. I like my office mate. He doesn't like me.

⊙ ____

7. Joseph has a brand-new **computer**. Joseph has a state-of-the-art cell phone. Joseph doesn't have a girlfriend.

⊙ ____

8. Sue doesn't **appreciate** getting up in the morning. Sue hates early-morning classes.

⊙ ____

9. Kang-suk is wearing big, black boots. He is wearing black pants. He is wearing a black shirt. He is wearing a black hat.

⊙ ____

10. Jung-eun may go to Thailand this summer. **Alternatively**, she may go to Europe.

⊙ ____

Subject – Verb Agreement

Read each sentence. If it contains an **error** in subject-verb agreement, write an SV on the line and correct the **error**. If the sentence is correct, write a C (correct) on the line.

1. _____ Animals was first **domesticated** about 7,000 years ago.
2. _____ **Globalization** have **created** both wealth and opportunities.
3. _____ It is very important to write down **assignments**, tests, and study times on a calendar.
4. _____ When **immigrants migrates** into a country, **infrastructure** must be built to **accommodate** them.
5. _____ After finding a good study **area**, you need to **concentrate** on only one particular **assignment**.
6. _____ **Interpreters**, who translates between languages, provide a valuable **mediation** service in business.

7. _____ You may have a hard time with this because you has not trained your mind to **focus** on only one thing.
8. _____ Anyone is **capable** of improving his or her study skills!
9. _____ As wine **matures**, its taste becomes smoother and more refined.
10. _____ Everyone's **objective** are the same: drive as quickly as possible without any regard for their fellow drivers.
11. _____ Many **revolutionaries** routinely **violate** the **norms** of the society around them.
12. _____ The **revenue** from the **Ministry** allow the class to **purchase** new books.

Noun and Pronoun Agreement

Fill in the space in each sentence with a pronoun that agrees with the given noun or nouns. More than one answer may be possible.

1. Mary and Bill are going together. We are going with _________.
2. Brad told me he lost his wallet, and I think I **found** _________.
3. As we were walking down the street, a car splashed water on the three of _________.
4. Because we **consult** regularly, there can be no problems between you and _________.
5. Because Paul and Jill passed the test, the Chairman appointed Paul and _________ to serve as officers.
6. The foremen permitted us to leave early, so _________ went drinking.
7. When the teacher **found** my book, she said, "Is this book _________?"
8. After we were arrested, the policemen requested _________ home addresses.
9. My girlfriend asked me, "Do you really love _________?"
10. Phil is wearing a big hat, and I think that is _________ coming down the road.

Prepositions

Fill in the blanks in the sentences below with the correct prepositions. Note to teachers. One fun way to preview this exercise is to divide the class up into **teams**, with one member at the board. Do the first few questions as a contest.

among	at	at	at	at	at	at	at	before	by	by
by	during	for	for	from	from	in	in	in	in	in
in	of	of	of	of	of	of	of	of	of	on
on	on	on	since	to	to	to	to	to	until	with

1. _____ 1961 _____ 1979, Park Chung Hee was president _____ South Korea.
2. Canada has a population density _____ 3.3 per square kilometer, according _____ **statistics released** _____ 2004.
3. George Washington was born _____ February 22, 1732, _____ the state _____ Virginia.
4. Sheila lives _____ 132 Wood Street, and her best friend Grace lives _____ Green Avenue. They both live _____ Toronto, Canada.
5. Please meet me _____ 6:00 pm _____ Monday. It's the last chance to meet _____ February.
6. _____ the University _____ Toronto, there is an excellent department _____ sociology.
7. **Located** _____ the east coast _____ Asia, Korea is separated _____ China _____ the Yellow Sea.
8. The **Federal** Building is **located** _____ the corner _____ State and Main.
9. Students sleeping _____ class is a big problem _____ Korean high schools.
10. His wife married him _____ his money.
11. Lee Seung didn't go _____ the USA; he learned English _____ an academy.
12. Park Chung Hee was assassinated _____ 1979 _____ the head _____ the KCIA.
13. If you eat dinner too early, you'll get hungry _____ you go _____ bed.
14. You must hand in your homework _____ Friday, or there will be a 10% penalty.
15. We have been in class _____ twenty minutes.

16. You have gone to school _____ the age _____ five.

17. I hate working _____ my summer vacation.

20. Please bring some money _____ you.

21. I am having trouble picking from _____ the **alternatives**.

22. I can't see you _____ I finish work.

23. Please don't make any modifications _____ my work.

Comparatives

Write sentences using comparatives and the cues given.

1. desk/(+)big/pencil

   ▶ ______________________________

2. Julia/(-)**intelligent**/Rebecca

   ▶ ______________________________

3. Seoul/(+)population/Busan

   ▶ ______________________________

4. dogs/(+)loud/cats

   ▶ ______________________________

5. wine glasses/(+) **stylish**/beer mugs

   ▶ ______________________________

6. Zeno/(-)lego puzzles/Thomas

   ▶ ______________________________

7. Canada/(+)lakes/Korea

   ▶ ______________________________

8. Korea/(+)long coast/Burma

   ▶ ______________________________

9. my cell phone/(-)**features**/your cell phone

   ▶ ______________________________

10. hamburgers/(+)calories/bibimbap

    ▶ ______________________________

Subordinating Conjunctions

Fill in the blanks in the sentences below with the correct subordinating conjunction. There may be more that one correct answer. Different answers may change the meaning of the sentence.

1. _________ the train was delayed for more than an hour, passengers were given a full refund..
2. I had to borrow money from my father _____________ I could start my own business.
3. __________ he was much younger than the others, he was the best soccer player on the **team**.
4. The video pauses ________ you press this button.
5. My brother chews gum ___________ he gets nervous.
6. I will not let you use my ball ___________ you let me play in the game.
7. Martha carefully cut the cake into slices ___________ everybody had their fair share.
8. ____________ his face was very familiar, I couldn't remember his name.
9. My landlady didn't mind me having parties _____________ my rent was paid on time.
10. My parents make me come home every night _________ the streetlamps turn on.

Dependent and Independent Clauses

Match the dependent and independent clauses. Note to teacher. One fun way to do this is to enlarge and photocopy these. Then cut them up into **individual** strips. Give one strip to each person in the class, and let them find their **partner**.

1. We could see very clearly _________
2. Violet read the newspaper _________
3. Although it is cold outside _________
4. Until her ankle heals _________
5. Ralph likes to sit by the window _________
6. If I had known you were coming _________

7. Because he was the first person to eat a piece of meat between two slices of bread _____

8. The room was filled with sound ______

9. Even though the chimney spewed black smoke and soot _____

10. When Professor Hubert announced that he had ordered chicken for everybody _____

a) _________ the students buzzed with excitement.
b) _________ I'd have baked a cake.
c) _________ because the moon was so bright.
d) _________ nobody complained to the **Environmental** Protection Agency.
e) _________ while Daisy walked in the woods.
f) _________ the sandwich was named after the Earl of Sandwich.
g) _________ our floor is very warm.
h) _________ after Joon turned on his stereo.
i) _________ Jin Hee can't play basketball.
j) _________ when he rides the bus.

Transition Expressions

Here is a partial list of transition expressions.

Relationship	Examples
addition	in addition, also, moreover, **furthermore**, as well, what is more, and
alternatives	**alternatively**, or
comparison	**similarly**, in the same way, **likewise**
concession	certainly, of course, to be sure, no doubt, although, even though, while, **notwithstanding**

consequence	therefore, thus, as a result, as a **consequence**, for this reason, so
difference	however, on the **contrary**, on the other hand, in **contrast**, but, unlike
emphasis	above all, especially, indeed, in fact, in particular, surely
example	for example, for instance
restatement	in other words
sequence	afterwards, at last, at present, currently, **eventually**, **finally**
similarities	**similarly**, **likewise**, in the same way, similar to
summary	in **conclusion**, to **summarize**, in **summary**, all in all, to **sum** up

Working with at least three of your classmates, **create** a story beginning with one of the following lines. Each person in order adds one sentence to the story, building upon what the **previous** person said. A **transition** expression must be used at the beginning of each sentence. Each story should have at least twelve lines. You cannot repeat any **transition** expressions within a story.

Example: It was a beautiful day.
Student 1: Therefore, Sally decided to go hiking.
Student 2: First, she put on her hiking clothes and a backpack.
Student 3: Next, she went to the subway station.
Student 1: However, when she got on the subway, she saw her old boyfriend

First Lines
1. It was a beautiful day.
2. Bill and Marie got on the airplane.
3. Sally suspected that her best friend, Joan, and her boyfriend, Mark, knew each

other too well.

4. I inherited $20,000,000 from my Uncle Ned.

Articles

Fill in the blanks with *a, an, the or X*, whichever is the most correct. Note to teachers. You might want to photocopy these and give a few questions to each group. Let them answer the questions, and then test the other students in the class.

1. I want ______ egg from that carton.
2. ______ house on _____corner has a blue roof.
3. Miss Kim speaks ______ Korean.
4. I borrowed ______ pencil from your pile of pencils and pens.
5. Min-Soo likes to play ______ baseball.
6. It was raining, so I bought ______ umbrella at_____subway station.
7. Please give me ______ cake on _____left.
8. I live on ______ Lake Street.
9. Seoul is_____capital of ______ Korea.
10. ______ apple_____day keeps_____doctor away.
11. Our neighbors have _____ cat and _____ dog. _____ cat is brown and ______ dog is white.
12. _____ children like _____ candy.
13. I come to _____ school by _____ subway. This morning, _____ subway was closed.
14. I have _____ pair of black shoes. _____ shoes are on _____ floor by _____ front door.
15. Driving lessons cost $20 _____ hour.
16. _____ wine comes from _____ grapes.
17. _____ Lake Superior, which is one of _____ Great Lakes, is _____ largest lake in _____ world.
18. We arrived in _____ Seoul on _____ third of August.
19. _____ Mount Halla is on _____ Cheju Island.

20. I went to _____ bed at 12:00 last night.

Fill in the blanks with *a, an, the or X*, whichever is the most correct.

_____ Foreigner in _____ Korea?

One day, I met _____ man on _____ subway who told me, "You are just like _____ Korean man." I first came to Korea in 1996, and I have been married to _____ Korean woman since 1998. I have _____ Korean mother-in-law, brother-in-law and two sisters-in-law. We go to their houses and visit their families. My son goes to _____ Korean elementary school, and I am concerned about his education. I am _____ lower-**intermediate** level Korean speaker, which means I can do most of _____ things I need to using _____ Korean language. Not only do I study _____ language, I also study _____ history and **culture**. I've been to _____ Cheju Island, Haeinsa, Kyungju, Seokcho, Wonju, Danyang, Chuncheon (I really like Kangwando) and various islands and other places in Korea too numerous to recount. I teach Korean students. I work with Koreans. I like _____ Korean food, especially hot, spicy soups like Kamjatang and Yookaejang. I take _____ bus and subway with Koreans, and I walk down _____ same crowded streets jostling with everybody else. Maybe that man was on to something.

Adjective Clauses

Combine the sentences by using adjective clauses.

1. Bongja Trot originated in Japan. It is the best music in Korea.
   ▶ ____
2. The new TV has arrived. We ordered the TV.
   ▶ ____

3. Mr. Jeens is our English teacher. He is bald.

▶ ______________________________

4. I wanted to see the movie. It was playing at 7:20.

▶ ______________________________

5. We saw some people. Their car had broken down.

▶ ______________________________

6. The girl just left. She had a big purse.

▶ ______________________________

7. Where is the cheese? It was in the refrigerator.

▶ ______________________________

8. I was looking for a book this morning. I've **found** it now.

▶ ______________________________

9. A cemetery is a spooky place. Dead people are buried there.

▶ ______________________________

10. Amanda has one son. She showed me a picture of him. He is a police officer.

▶ ______________________________

Appendix 3 : The Academic Word List[1)]

Here a list of the most common words used in academic English, as compiled by Averil Coxhead at Victoria University in Wellington, New Zealand. These are given in their noun, verb, adjective and adverb forms. The most common form of the word is found in italics. Only American spellings have been utilized.

Noun	Verb	Adjective	Adverb
abandon/abandonment	abandon/abandoned/ abandoning/abandons	abandoned	x
abstract/abstracts/ abstraction/abstractions	x	*abstract*	abstractly
academia/*academic*/ academics/ academies/academy	x	*academic*	academically
access/accesses/ accessibility	*access*/accessed/accesses/ accessing	accessible/ inaccessible	x
accommodation	accommodate/accommodated/ accommodates/ accommodating	accommodating	x
accompaniment	*accompanied*/accompanies/ accompany/accompanying	accompanying/ unaccompanied	x
accumulation	accumulate/accumulated/ accumulates/accumulating	accumulated/ accumulating	x
accuracy/inaccuracies/ inaccuracy	x	*accurate*/inaccurate	accurately
achievement/achievements	*achieve*/achieved/ achieves/achieving	achievable/achieved	x
acknowledgement/ acknowledgements	acknowledge/*acknowledged*/ acknowledges/acknowledging	acknowledged	x
acquisition/acquisitions	acquire/acquired/ acquires/acquiring	acquired/acquiring	x
adaptability/adaptation/ adaptations	adapt/adapted/ adapting/adapts	adaptable/adaptive	x
adequacy/inadequacies/ inadequacy	x	*adequate*/inadequate	adequately/ inadequately
x	x	*adjacent*	x
adjustment/adjustments readjustment/readjustments	adjust/adjusted/adjusting/ adjusts/readjust/readjusted/ readjusting/readjusts	adjusted/adjusting/ readjusted	x

1)DAveril Coxhead. Most Frequent Words of the Academic Word List in Sublists. Victoria University School of Applied Language Studies. n.d. http://www.victoria.ac.nz/lals/staff/Averil.coxhead/awl/download/awlfrequent.pdf

administration/ administrations/ administrator/ administrators	administrate/ administrates	administrative	administratively
adult/*adults*/adulthood	x	adult	x
advocate/advocates/ advocacy	*advocate*/advocated/ advocates/advocating	x	x
x	*affect*/affected/affecting/affects	affected/affective/ unaffected	affectively
aggregate/aggregation	*aggregate*/aggregated/ aggregates/aggregating	*aggregate*/aggregated	x
aid	*aid*/aided/aiding/aids	aided/unaided	x
x	x	x	albeit
allocation/allocations	allocate/allocated/ allocates/allocating	allocated	x
alternate/alteration/ alterations	*alter*/altered/altering/alters	alterable/altered/ altering/alternating/ unaltered/unalterable	x
alternative/alternatives	x	*alternative*	alternatively
ambiguities/ambiguity	x	*ambiguous*/ unambiguous	unambiguously
amendment/amendments	amend/amended/ amending/amends	amended	x
analogies/analogy	x	*analogous*	x
analysis/analyst/analysts	analyze/analyzed/ analyzes/analyzing	analytic/analytical	analytically
x	x	*annual*	annually
anticipation	anticipate/*anticipated*/ anticipates/anticipating	*anticipated*/ unanticipated	x
x	x	apparent	apparently
appendices/*appendix*	append/appended/ appending/appends	appended	x
appreciation	appreciate/appreciated/ appreciates/appreciating	appreciable/ unappreciated	appreciably
approach	*approach*/approached/ approaches/approaching	approachable/ unapproachable	x
appropriacy/ appropriateness/ inappropriacy/ inappropriateness	x	*appropriate*/ inappropriate	appropriately/ inappropriately
approximation/ approximations	approximate/*approximated*/ approximates/approximating	approximate	approximately
arbitrariness	x	arbitrary	arbitrarily
area/areas	x	x	x
aspect/aspects	x	x	x
assemblies/*assembly*	assemble/assembled/ assembles/assembling	assembled	x

assessment/reassessment	assess/assessed/assesses/assessing/reassess/reassessed/reassessing	assessable/assessed/assessing/reassessed/unassessed	x
assignment/assignments	assign/assigned/assigning/assigns/reassign/reassigned/reassigning/reassigns	assigned/assigning/reassigned/reassigning/unassigned	x
assistance/assistant/assistants	assist/assisted/assisting/assists	assisted/assisting/unassisted	x
assumption/assumptions	*assume*/assumed/assumes/assuming	assumed	x
assurance/assurances	assure/*assured*/assures/assuring	assured/assuring	assuredly
attachment/attachments	attach/attached/ attaches/attaching/unattached	attached/unattached	x
attainment/attainments	attain/*attained*/attaining/attains	attainable/*attained*/unattainable	x
attitude/*attitudes*	x	x	x
attribute/attributes/attribution	attribute/*attributed*/attributes/attributing	attributable	x
author	*author*/authored/authoring/authors	x	x
authority/authorities	x	authoritative	x
automation	automate/automated/automates/automating	automated/automatic	*automatically*
availability	x	*available*/unavailable	x
awareness	x	*aware*/unaware	x
behalf	x	x	x
beneficiary/beneficiaries/*benefit*/benefits	*benefit*/benefited/benefiting/benefits	beneficial/benefiting	x
bias	*bias*/biased/biases/biasing	biased/unbiased	x
bond	*bond*/bonded/bonding/bonds	bonded/bonding	x
brevity/*brief*/briefs	*brief*/briefed/briefing/briefs	*brief*/briefed/briefing	briefly
bulk	*bulk*	bulky	x
capability/capabilities	x	*capable*/incapable	x
capacity/capacities	incapacitate/incapacitated	incapacitated	x
categorization/*categories*/category	categorize/categorized/categorizes/categorizing	categorized/categorizing	x
x	cease/ceased/*ceases*/ceasing	ceaseless	x
challenge/challenger/challengers	*challenge*/challenged/challenges/challenging	challenged/challenging	x
channel/channels	*channel*/channeled/channeling/channels	channeled	x
chapter/chapters	x	x	x
chart	chart/charted/charting/charts	charted/uncharted	x
chemical/chemicals	x	*chemical*	chemically

circumstance/*circumstances*	x	x	x
citation/citations	cite/*cited*/citing/cites	*cited*/citing	x
x	x	*civil*	x
clarification/*clarity*	clarified/clarifies/ clarify/clarifying	clarified/clarifying	x
classic/classics	x	classic/*classical*	x
clause/clauses	x	x	x
code/codes	code/coded/codes/coding	coded	x
coherence	x	coherent/incoherent	coherently/ incoherently
coincidence/coincidences	*coincide*/coincided/ coincides/coinciding	coincident/ coincidental	x
collapse	*collapse*/collapsed/ collapses/collapsing	collapsed/collapsing	x
colleague/*colleagues*	x	x	x
commencement	commence/*commenced*/ commences/commencing recommence/recommenced/ recommencing	x	x
comment/*comments*/ commentaries/commentary/ commentator/commentators	comment/commented/ commenting/*comments*	x	x
commission/commissioner/ commissioners	*commission*/commissioned/ commissioning/commissions	commissioned/ commissioning	x
commitment/commitments	commit/commits/ committed/committing	committed	x
commodities/*commodity*	x	x	x
communication/ communications	communicate/communicated/ communicates/communicating	communicable/ communicating/ communicative/ uncommunicative	communicatively
communities/community	x	x	x
compatibility/incompatibility	x	compatible/ *incompatible*	x
compensation/compensations	compensate/*compensated*/ compensates/compensating	compensatory	x
compilation/compilations	compile/compiled/ compiles/compiling	*compiled*	x
complement/complements	*complement*/complemented/ complementing/complements	complementary	x
complex/complexities/ complexity	x	complex	x
component/componentry/ *components*	x	x	x
compound/*compounds*	compound/compounded/ compounding/*compounds*	compound	x
x	x	*comprehensive*	comprehensively
x	*comprise*/comprised/ comprises/comprising	x	x

computation/computations/ *computer*/computers	compute/computed/ computing/computerized	computable/ computational/ computerized/ computing	x
x	conceive/*conceived*/ conceives/conceiving	conceivable/*conceived*/ inconceivable	conceivably/ inconceivably
concentration	concentrate/concentrated/ concentrates/concentrating	concentrated/ concentrating	x
concept/conception/ concepts/conceptualization	conceptualize/conceptualized/ conceptualizes/conceptualizing	conceptual	conceptually
conclusion/conclusions	conclude/concluded/ concludes/concluding	concluding/ conclusive/ inconclusive	conclusively/ inconclusively
x	x	concurrent	*concurrently*
conduct	*conduct*/conducted/ conducting/conducts	conducting	x
conference/conferences	confer/conferred/ conferring/confers	conferring	x
confinement/confines	confine/*confined*/ confines/confining	confined/confining/ unconfined	x
confirmation	confirm/*confirmed*/ confirming/confirms	*confirmed*/confirming	x
conflict/conflicts	*conflict*/conflicted/ conflicting/conflicts	conflicted/conflicting	x
conformability/conformance/ conformation/conformist/ conformists/*conformity*/ nonconformist/ nonconformists/nonconformity	conform/conformed/ conforming/conforms	conforming	x
consensus/*consent*	*consent*/consented/ consenting/consents	consenting	x
consequence/*consequences*	x	consequent	consequently
x	consider/considered considering/considers	considerable	considerably
consistency/inconsistency/ inconsistencies	consist/consisted/ consisting/consists	*consistent*/inconsistent	consistently
constant/constants/ constancy/inconstancy	x	*constant*	constantly/ inconstantly
consistencies/constituency/ constituent /constituents/ constitution/constitutions	constitute/constituted/ constitutes/constituting	constitutional/ constitutive/ unconstitutional	constitutionally
constraint/*constraints*	constrain/constrained/ constraining/constrains	constrained/ constraining/ unconstrained	x
construction/constructions/ constructor/reconstruction	construct/constructed/ constructing/constructs reconstruct/reconstructed/ reconstructing/reconstructs	constructed/ constructional/ constructive/ reconstructed/ reconstructiv	x
consultancy/consultant/ consultants/*consultation*/ consultations	consult/consulted/ consulting/consults	consulting/ consultative	x

consumer/consumers/ consumption	consume/consumed/ consumes/consuming	consumed/consuming	x
contact/contacts	*contact*/contacted/ contacting/contacts	contactable	x
contemporaries/*contemporary*	x	*contemporary*	x
context/contexts	contextualize/contextualized/ contextualizing/ uncontextualized	contextual/ contextualized/ uncontextualized	contextually
contract/contracts/ contractor/contractors	*contract*/contracted/ contracting/	contracted/ contracting	x
contradiction/contradictions	contradict/contradicted/ contradicting/contradicts	contradictory	x
x	x	*contrary*	contrarily
contrast/contrasts	*contrast*/contrasted/ contrasting/contrasts	contrasting/ contrastive	x
contribution/contributions/ contributor/contributors	contribute/contributed/ contributes/contributing	contributing	x
controversies/*controversy*	x	controversial/ uncontroversial	controversially
convention/conventions	convene/convenes/ convened/convening	conventional/ unconventional	conventionally
converse	converse	converse	*conversely*
conversion/conversions/ convert/converts	convert/converted/*converting*/ converts	*converted*/convertible	x
x	convince/*convinced*/ convinces/convincing	*convinced*/convincing/ unconvinced	convincingly
cooperative/cooperation	cooperate/cooperated/ cooperates/cooperating	cooperating/ *cooperative*	cooperatively
coordinate/coordination/ coordinator/coordinators	coordinate/coordinated/ coordinates/coordinating	coordinate/ coordinated/ coordinating	x
core/cores	*core*/cored/coring	*core*/cored	x
corporation/corporations	x	*corporate*	x
correspondence	correspond/corresponded/ *corresponding*/corresponds	*corresponding*	correspondingly
couple/couples	*couple*/coupled/coupling/ couples	coupled/coupling	x
creation/creations/creativity/ creator/creators	*create*/created/creates/creating/ recreate/recreated/recreates/ recreating	created/creating/ creative/recreated	creatively
credit/credits/creditor/creditors	*credit*/credited/crediting	credited/creditable	creditably
criteria/criterion	x	x	x
x	x	*crucial*	crucially
culture/cultures	culture/cultured/cultures	cultural/cultured/ uncultured	culturally
currencies/*currency*	x	x	x
cycle/cycles	*cycle*/cycled/cycles/cycling	cyclic/cyclical	x
data	x	x	x
debate	*debate*/debated/debates/ debating	debatable/debating	x
decade/*decades*	x	x	x

decline/declines	*decline*/declined/ declines/declining	declining	x
deduction/deductions	deduce/deduced/ deduces/deducing	deduced	x
definition/definitions	define/defined/defines/ defining/ redefine/redefined/ redefines/redefining	definable/defined/ defining/redefined/ redefining/undefined	x
x	x	*definite* /definitive/ indefinite	definitely/indefinitely
demonstration/demonstrator/ demonstrators	*demonstrate*/demonstrated/ demonstrates/demonstrating	demonstrable/ demonstrated/ demonstrating/ demonstrative	demonstrably/ demonstratively
denotation/denotations	*denote*/denoted/ denotes/denoting	x	x
denial/denials	*deny*/denied/denies/denying	deniable/undeniable	x
depression	depress/depressed/ depresses/depressing	depressed/depressing	x
derivative/derivatives/ derivation/derivations/	derive/*derived*/derives/deriving	derivative/derived	x
design/designs/ designer/designers	*design*/designed/ designing/designs	designed/designing	x
detection/detective/ detectives/detector/detectors	detect/*detected*/ detecting/detects	detectable/*detected*/ detecting	x
deviation/deviations	deviate/deviated/ deviates/deviating	x	x
device/devices	x	x	x
devotion/devotions	devote/*devoted*/ devotes/devoting	*devoted*	devotedly
differentiation	differentiate/differentiated/ differentiates/differentiating	differentiated	x
dimension/*dimensions*	x	dimensional/ multidimensional	x
diminution	diminish/*diminished*/ diminishes/diminishing	*diminished*/ diminishing/ undiminished	x
discretion/indiscretion	x	discretediscretionary/ indiscrete	discretely
discrimination	discriminate/discriminated/ discriminates/discriminating	discriminating	x
displacement	displace/displaced/ displaces/displacing	displaced/displacing	x
display	*display*/displayed/ displaying/displays	displayed/displaying	x
disposal	dispose/disposed/ disposes/disposing	disposed/disposable	x
distinction/distinctions distinctiveness	x	distinct/distinctive/ indistinct	distinctly/ distinctively/ indistinctly

distortion/distortions	distort/*distorted*/ distorting/distorts	*distorted*/distorting	x
distribution/distributions/ distributor/distributors redistribution	distribute/distributed/ distributing/redistribute/ redistributed/redistributes/ redistributing	distributed/ distributing/ distributional/ distributive/ redistributed/ redistributing	x
diversification/*diversity*	diversified/diversifies/ diversify/diversifying	diverse/diversified	diversely
document/documents documentation	*document*/documented/ documenting/documents	documented/ documenting	x
domain/domains	x	x	x
domestic/domestics	domesticate/domesticated/ domesticating	*domestic*/domesticated	domestically
dominance/domination	dominate/dominated/ dominates/dominating	*dominant*/dominated/ dominating	x
draft/drafts	*draft*/drafted/drafting/drafts/ redraft/redrafted/ redrafting/redrafts	*draft*/drafted/drafting/ redrafted	x
drama/dramas/dramatist/ dramatists/dramatization/ dramatizations	dramatize/dramatized/ dramatizes/dramatizing	*dramatic*	dramatically
duration	x	x	x
dynamics	x	dynamic	dynamically
economics/economist/ economists/economies/ economy	economize	*economic*/economical/ economy/ uneconomical	economically
edition/editions/editor/ editorial/editorials/editors	edit/edited/editing/edits	edited/editing/ editorial	x
element/elements	x	x	x
elimination	*eliminate*/eliminated/ eliminates/eliminating	x	x
emergence	emerge/emerged/ emerges/emerging	emergent/emerging	x
emphasis	emphasize/emphasized/ emphasizes/emphasizing	emphasized/emphatic	emphatically
empiricism	x	*empirical*	empirically
x	*enable*/enabled/enables/ enabling	enabling	x
encounter	encounter/encountered/ encountering/encounters	x	x
energies/*energy*	x	energetic	energetically
enforcement	enforce/enforced/ enforces/enforcing	enforced	x
enhancement	enhance/*enhanced*/ enhances/enhancing	*enhanced*/enhancing	x
enormity	x	*enormous*	enormously
x	*ensure*/ensured/ ensures/ensuring	x	x
entity/*entities*	x	x	x

environment/environments/ environmentalist/ environmentalists	x	environmental	environmentally
equation/equations	equate/equated/ equates/equating	x	x
equipment	equip/equipped/ equipping/equips	equipped	x
equivalence/*equivalent*	x	*equivalent*	x
erosion	erode/eroded/erodes/eroding	eroded/eroding	x
error/errors	x	erroneous	erroneously
establishment/establishments/ disestablishment	establish/*established*/ establishes/ establishing/disestablish/ disestablished/disestablishes/ disestablishing	*established*/ establishing/ disestablished/ disestablishing	x
estate/estates	x	x	x
estimate/estimation/ estimations/ overestimate/underestimate	*estimate*/estimated/estimates/ estimating/overestimate/ overestimated/overestimates/ overestimating/underestimate/ underestimated/ underestimates/ underestimating	estimable/estimated/ overestimated/ underestimated	x
ethic/ethics	x	*ethical*/unethical	ethically
ethnic/ethnicity	x	*ethnic*	x
evaluation/evaluations/ re-evaluation	evaluate/evaluated/evaluates/ evaluating/re-evaluate/ re-evaluated/re-evaluates/ re-evaluating	evaluated/evaluative/ re-evaluated	x
eventuality	x	eventual	*eventually*
evidence	x	evident/evidential	evidently
evolution/evolutionist/ evolutionists	evolve/evolved/ evolves/evolving	evolved/evolving/ evolutionary	x
x	*exceed*/exceeded/ exceeding/exceeds	exceeding	x
exclusion/exclusionist/ exclusions	exclude/*excluded*/ excludes/excluding	*excluded*/exclusionary/ exclusive	exclusively
exhibit/exhibition/ exhibitions	*exhibit*/exhibited/ exhibiting/exhibits	exhibited/exhibiting	x
expansion/expansionism	expand/expanded/ expanding/expands	expanded/expanding/ expansive	x
expert/experts/expertise	x	*expert*	expertly
x	x	*explicit*	explicitly
exploit/*exploitation*	exploit/exploited/ exploiting/exploits	exploited/exploiting	x
export/exports/ exporter/exporters	*export*/exported/exporting	exported/exporting	x
exposure/exposures	expose/exposed/ exposes/exposing	exposed	x
externality/externalization	externalize/externalized/ externalizes/externalizing	*external*	externally

extract/extracts/ extraction	*extract*/extracted/ extracting/extracts	x	x
facilitation/facilities/facilitator/ facilitators/facility	*facilitate*/facilitated/ facilitates/facilitating	x	x
factor/*factors*	factor/factored/factoring	x	x
feature/*features*	feature/featured/ *features*/featuring	featured	x
federation/federations	x	*federal*/federated	x
fee/*fees*	x	x	x
file/files	file/filed/files/filing	filed/filing	x
final/finals/finality	finalize/finalized/ finalizes/finalizing	*final*/finalized	finally
finances/financier/ financiers/financing	finance/financed/finances/ financing	*financial*/financed/ financing	financially
x	x	*finite*/infinite	infinitely
flexibility/inflexibility	x	flexible/inflexible	x
fluctuation/*fluctuations*	fluctuate/fluctuated/ fluctuates/fluctuating	fluctuating	x
focus	*focus*/focused/focuses/ focusing/refocus/refocused/ refocuses/refocusing	focused/focusing/ refocused/refocusing	x
format	*format*/formatted/ formatting/formats	formatted	x
formula/formulae/formulas/ formulation/formulations/ reformulation/reformulations	formulate/formulated/ formulating/reformulate/ reformulated/reformulating	x	x
x	x	*forthcoming*	x
founder/founders	found/*founded*/founding	*founded*/founding/ unfounded	
foundation/foundations	x	x	x
framework/frameworks	x	x	x
function	function/functioned/ functioning/functions	functional/ functioning/ functionless	functionally
fund/funder/funding/*funds*	fund/funded/funding/*funds*	funded/funding	x
fundamental	x	*fundamental*	fundamentally
x	x	x	*furthermore*
gender/genders	x	gendered	x
generator	generate/*generated*/ generates/generating	*generated*/generating	x
generation/generations	x	x	x
globe/globalization	globalize/globalizing/ globalized/globalizes	global	globally
goal/*goals*	x	x	x
grade/grades	*grade*/graded/grades/grading	graded	x
grant/grants	grant/*granted*/granting/grants	x	x
guarantee	*guarantee*/guaranteed/		
guaranteeing/guarantees	guaranteed	x	
guideline/*guidelines*	x	x	x
x	x	x	*hence*
hierarchies/hierarchy	x	*hierarchical*	x

highlight/highlights	highlight/*highlighted*/ highlighting/highlights	*highlighted*/ highlighting	x
hypotheses/*hypothesis*	hypothesize/hypothesized/ hypothesizes/hypothesizing	hypothetical	hypothetically
x	x	*identical*	identically
identification/identity/ identities	identified/identifies/ identify/identifying	identifiable/*identified*/ identifying/ unidentifiable	x
ideologies/*ideology*	x	ideological	ideologically
ignorance	ignore/*ignored*/ignores/ ignoring	ignorant	x
illustration/illustrations	illustrate/*illustrated*/ illustrates/illustrating	*illustrated*/illustrating/ illustrative	x
image/imagery/images	x	x	x
immigrant/immigrants/ *immigration*	immigrate/immigrates/ immigrated/immigrating	x	x
impact	*impact*/impacted/ impacting/impacts	impacted	x
implement/*implementation*/ implements	implement/implemented/ implementing/implements	x	x
implication/*implications*	implicate/implicated/ implicates/implicating	x	x
x	x	implicit	implicitly
x	implied/*implies*/implying/ imply	implied	x
imposition	impose/*imposed*/ imposes/imposing	imposing	x
incentive/incentives	x	x	x
incidence/incident/incidents	x	x	incidentally
inclination/inclinations	incline/inclined/inclines/ inclining	inclined	x
income/incomes	x	x	x
incorporation	incorporate/*incorporated*/ incorporates/incorporating	*incorporated*	x
index	*index*/indexed/indexes/ indexing	indexed/indexing	x
indication/indications/ indicator/indicators	*indicate*/indicated/ indicates/indicating	*indicated*/indicating/ indicative	x
individual/*individuals*/ individualism/individualist/ individualists/individuality	individualized	*individual*/ individualistic	individually
induction	induce/*induced*/induces/ inducing	*induced*/inducing	x
inevitability	x	inevitable	*inevitably*
inference/inferences	infer/*inferred*/inferring/infers	inferred	x
infrastructure/infrastructures	x	x	x
x	x	*inherent*	inherently
inhibition/inhibitions	inhibit/inhibited/ inhibiting/inhibits	inhibited/inhibiting	x
initial	*initial*	*initial*	initially

initiate/initiation/initiations/ initiative/*initiatives*/initiator/ initiators	initiate/initiated/ initiates/initiating	x	x
injury/injuries	injure/injured/ injures/injuring	injured/uninjured	x
innovation/innovations/ innovator/innovators	innovate/innovated/ innovates/innovating	innovative	x
input/inputs	*input*/inputs	x	x
insert/insertion	*insert*/inserted/inserting/inserts	inserted	x
insight/*insights*	x	insightful	x
inspection/inspections inspector/inspectors	inspect/inspected/ inspecting/inspects	inspected/inspecting	x
instance/instances	x	x	x
institute/institutes/institution/ institutions/institutionalism	*institute*/instituted/institutes/ instituting/institutionalize/ institutionalized/ institutionalizes/ institutionalizing	institutional/ institutionalized/ institutionalizing	institutionally
instruction/*instructions* instructor/instructors	instruct/instructed/ instructing/instructs	instrutional instructive	x
x	x	*integral*	x
integration	integrate/integrated/ integrates/integrating	integrated/ integrating/	x
integrity	x	x	x
intelligence	x	intelligent/ unintelligent	intelligently
intenseness/intensification/ intension/*intensity*	intensified/intensifies/ intensify/intensifying	intense/intensified/ intensive/intensifying	intensely/intensively
interaction	interact/interacted/ interacting/interacts	interacting/interactive	interactively
intermediate	x	*intermediate*	x
x	internalize/internalized/ internalizes/internalizing	*internal*	internally
interpreter/*interpretation*/ interpretations/ misinterpretation/ misinterpretations/ reinterpretation reinterpretations	interpret/interpreted/ interpreting/interprets/ misinterpret/misinterpreting/ misinterprets/ reinterpret/reinterpreted/ reinterprets/reinterpreting	interpreted/ interpreting/ interpretive/ misinterpreted/ misinterpreting/ reinterpreted/ reinterpreting	x
interval/intervals	x	x	x
intervention/interventions	intervene/intervened/ intervenes/intervening	intervening	x
x	x	*intrinsic*	intrinsically
investment/investments/ investor/investors/ reinvestment	invest/invested/investing/ invests/reinvest/reinvested/ reinvesting/reinvests/disnvest	invested/investing/ reinvested/ reinvesting	x
investigation/investigations investigator/investigators	investigate/investigated/ investigates/investigating	investigative/ investigated/ investigating	x
x	invoke/*invoked*/invokes/ invoking	x	x

involvement	involve/*involved*/involving/involves	*involved*/uninvolved	x
isolation/isolationism	isolate/*isolated*/isolates/isolating	*isolated*/isolating	x
issue/*issues*	issue/issued/*issues*/issuing	issued/issuing	x
item/itemization/*items*	itemize/itemized/itemizes/itemizing	itemized/itemizing	x
job/jobs	x	x	x
journal/journals	x	x	x
justification/justifications	justified/justifies/justify/justifying	justified/justifiable/unjustified	justifiably
label/labels	*label*/labeled/labeling/labels	labeled/labeling	x
labor/labors/laborer	*labor*/labored/labors/laboring	labored/laboring	x
layer/layering	*layer*/layered/layering/layers	layered	x
lecture/lectures/lecturer/lecturers	*lecture*/lectured/lectures/lecturing	x	x
legality/illegality	x	*legal*/illegal	legally/illegally
legislation/legislator/legislators/legislature	legislate/legislated/legislates/legislating	legislated/legislating/legislative	x
levies/*levy*	levies/*levy*	x	x
liberal/liberalism/liberalization/liberation/liberations/liberator/liberators/liberals	liberalize/liberalized/liberalizes/liberalizing liberate/liberated/liberates/liberating	*liberal*/liberalized/liberalizing/liberated/liberating	liberally
license/licenses	*license*/licensed/licenses/licensing	licensable/licensed/licensing/unlicensed	x
x	x	x	*likewise*
link/linkage/linkages	*link*/linked/linking/links	linked/linking	x
location/relocation	locate/located/locating/relocate/relocated/relocates/relocating	located/relocated	x
logic/logician/logicians	x	logical/illogical	logically/illogically
maintenance	maintain/maintained/maintaining/maintains	maintained	x
major/majority/majorities	*major*	*major*	x
manipulation/manipulations	manipulate/manipulated/manipulates/manipulating	manipulative/manipulated/manipulating	x
manual/manuals	x	*manual*	manually
margin/margins	x	*marginal*	marginally
maturation/maturity/immaturity	*mature*/matured/matures/maturing	*mature*/matured/maturing/maturational/immature	x
max/*maximum*/maximization	maximize/maximized/maximizes/maximizing	maximizing/*maximum*	maximally
mechanism/mechanisms	x	x	x
media	x	x	x
mediation	mediate/mediated/mediates/mediating	mediated/mediating	x
medical	x	medical	medically

medium	x	*medium*	x
mentality	x	*mental*	mentally
method/methods/ methodologies/methodology	x	methodical/ methodological	x
migrant/migrants/ *migration*/migrations	migrate/migrated/ migrates/migrating	migrating/migratory	x
military	x	*military*	x
minimalist/minimalists minimalism/ minimalization	minimalize/*minimalized*/ minimalizes/minimalizing	*minimal*/minimalist/ minimalistic/ minimalized/ minimalizing	minimally
x	minimize/minimized/ minimizes/minimizing	minimized	x
minimum	x	*minimum*	x
ministries/*ministry*	ministered/ministering	ministerial	x
minor/minority/ *minorities*/minors	minor/minors	minor	x
mode/modes	x	x	x
modification/modifications	*modified*/modifies/ modify/modifying	*modified*/modifying/ unmodified	x
monitor	monitor/monitored/ *monitoring*/monitors	monitored/ *monitoring*/ unmonitored	x
motivation/motivations motive/motives	motivate/motivated/ motivates/motivating	motive/motivated/ motivating/ unmotivated	x
x	x	mutual	mutually
negative/negatives	negate/negated/ negates/negating	*negative*	negatively
network/networks	*network*/networked/ networking/networks	x	x
neutral/neutrality/ neutralization	neutralize/neutralized/ neutralizes/neutralizing	*neutral*/neutralized/ neutralizing	x
x	x	x	*nevertheless*
x	x	x	*nonetheless*
norm/*norms*	x	x	x
normality/normalization	normalize/normalized/ normalizes/normalizing	*normal*/normalized/ abnormal	normally/abnormally
notion/notions	x	x	x
x	x	x	*notwithstanding*
x	x	*nuclear*	x
objective/objectivity	x	*objective*	objectively
x	obtain/*obtained*/obtaining/ obtains	obtainable/*obtained*/ unobtainable	x
x	x	*obvious*	obviously
occupancy/occupant/occupants occupation/occupations/ occupier/occupiers	occupied/occupies/ occupy/occupying	*occupational*/occupied/ occupying	x

occurrence/occurrences	*occur*/occurred/occurring/occurs/reoccur/reoccurred/reoccurring/reoccurs	occurring/reoccurring	x
odds	x	*odd*	x
offset/offsets	*offset*/offsets/offsetting	offsetting	x
x	x	*ongoing*	x
option/options	x	optional	x
orientation/reorientation	orient/orientate/orientated/orientates/orientating/oriented/orienting/orients/reorient	orientated/reoriented	x
outcome/*outcomes*	x	x	x
output/outputs	*output*/outputs	x	x
x	x	*overall*	*overall*
overlap	*overlap*/overlapped/overlapping/overlaps	overlapped/overlapping	x
overseas	x	overseas	overseas
panel/paneling	*panel*/paneled/paneling/panels	paneled	x
paradigm/paradigms	x	x	x
paragraph/paragraphs	*paragraph*/paragraphing/paragraphs	x	x
parallel/parallels	*parallel*/paralleled/paralleling/parallels	*parallel*/unparalleled	x
parameter/*parameters*	x	x	x
participant/participants/*participation*	participate/participated/	participating/participatory	x
partner/partners/*partnership*/partnerships	partner	x	x
passivity	x	*passive*	passively
perception/perceptions	perceive/*perceived*/perceives/perceiving	*perceived*	x
percent/percentage/percentages	x	x	*percent*
period/periods/periodical/periodicals	x	*period*/periodic/periodical	periodically
persistence	persist/persisted/persisting/persists	*persistent*	persistently
perspective/perspectives	x	x	x
phase/phases	*phase*/phased/phases/phasing	phased	x
phenomenon/phenomena	x	phenomenal	x
philosopher/philosophers/philosophies/*philosophy*	philosophize/philosophized/philosophizes/philosophizing	philosophical	philosophically
physical/physicality	x	*physical*	physically
plus/pluses	x	*plus*	x
policy/policies	x	x	x
portion/portions	*portion*	x	x
pose	pose/*posed*/poses/posing	x	x
positive	x	*positive*	positively
potential	x	*potential*	potentially
practitioner/*practitioners*	x	x	x
precedence/precedent	precede/preceded/precedes/*preceding*	*preceding*/unprecedented	x

precision	x	*precise*/imprecise	precisely
predictability/prediction/ predictions/unpredictability	predict/predicted/ predicting/predicts	predictable/ predicted/ predicting/ unpredictable/ predctive	x
predominance	predominate/predominated/ predominates/predominating	predominant	*predominantly*
preliminaries/*preliminary*	x	*preliminary*	x
presumption/presumptions	presume/presumed/ presumes/presuming	presumed/ presumptuous	presumably
x	x	*previous*	previously
x	x	*primary*	primarily
primacy	x	*prime*	x
principal	x	*principal*	principally
principle/principles	x	principled/ unprincipled	x
x	x	*prior*	x
priorities/*priority*/ prioritization	prioritize/prioritized/ prioritizes/prioritizing	x	x
proceeding/*procedure*/ procedures/proceeds	proceed/proceeded/ proceeding/proceedings/ proceeds	proceeding/ procedural	x
process	*process*/processed/processes/ processing	processed/processing	x
professional/professionals/ professionalism	x	*professional*	professionally
prohibition/prohibitions	prohibit/*prohibited*/ prohibiting/prohibits	*prohibited*/prohibitive	x
project/projection/projections	*project*/projected/ projecting/projects	projected/projecting	x
promotion/promotions promoter/promoters	*promote*/promoted/ promotes/promoting	promoted	x
proportion/proportions/ disproportion	*proportion*/proportions	proportional/ disproportionate	proportionally/ proportionately/ disproportionately
prospect/prospects	*prospect*/prospects	prospective	x
protocol/protocols	x	x	x
psychology/psychologist/ psychologists	x	psychological	psychologically
publication/publications	x	x	x
publisher/publishers	publish/*published*/ publishes/publishing	*published*/publishing/ unpublished	x
purchase/purchaser/ purchasers	*purchase*/purchased/ purchases/purchasing	purchased/ purchasing	x
pursuit/pursuits	*pursue*/pursued/ pursues/pursuing	x	x
x	x	*qualitative*	qualitatively
quotation/quotations/ quote/quotes	quote/quoted/ quotes/quoting	quoted	x
radical/radicals	x	*radical*	radically

randomness	x	*random*	randomly
range	*range*/ranged/ranges/ranging	x	x
ratio/ratios	x	x	x
rationalism/rationality/ rationalization/rationalizations	rationalize/rationalized/ rationalizes/rationalizing	*rational*/irrational	rationally
reaction/reactions/ reactionaries/reactionary/ reactivation/reactor/reactors	react/reacted/reacting/ reactivate/reacts	reacting/reactive	x
recovery	recover/recovered/ recovering/recovers	recoverable/ recovered/ recovering	x
refinement/refinements	*refine*/refined/refines/refining	refined	x
regime/regimes	x	x	x
region/regions	regionalize/regionalized/ regionalizes/regionalizing	regional	regionally
register/registers/ registration/deregistration	register/*registered*/registering/ registers/deregister/ deregistered/deregistering/ deregisters	*registered*/registering/ deregistered	x
regulation/*regulations*/ regulator/regulators/ deregulation	regulate/regulated/regulates/ regulating/deregulated/ deregulates/deregulating/	regulated/regulatory/ deregulated/ unregulated	x
reinforcement/reinforcements	reinforce/reinforced/ reinforces/reinforcing	*reinforced*/reinforcing	x
reject/rejects/rejection	reject/*rejected*/rejecting/rejects	*rejected*	x
relaxation	relax/*relaxed*/relaxes/relaxing	*relaxed*/relaxing	x
release/releases	release/released/releases/ releasing	released	x
relevance/irrelevance	x	*relevant*/irrelevant	x
reliability/*reliance*	rely/relied/relies/relying	reliable/reliant/ unreliable	reliably
reluctance	x	*reluctant*	reluctantly
removal/removals/remove	remove/*removed*/ removes/removing	*removed*/removable	x
requirement/requirements	require/*required*/requires/ requiring	*required*	x
research/researches/ researcher/researchers	*research*/researched/ researches/researching	researched	x
residence/*resident*/residents	reside/resided/resides/residing	*resident*/residential/ residing	x
resolution/resolve	resolve/resolved/ resolves/resolving	resolved/unresolved	x
resource/*resources*/	resource/resourced/ *resources*/resourcing	resourceful/ under-resourced/ unresourceful	x
response/responses/respondent/ respondents/responsiveness	respond/responded/ responding/responds	responding/ responsive/ unresponsive	x
restoration	*restore*/restored/ restores/restoring	restored/restoring	x

restraint/*restraints*	restrain/restrained/ restraining/restrains	restrained/ restraining/ unrestrained	x
restriction/restrictions	restrict/*restricted*/ restricting/restricts	*restricted*/restricting/ restrictive unrestricted/ unrestrictive	restrictively
retainer/retainers retention	retain/*retained*/ retaining/retains	*retained*/retaining/ retentive	x
revelation/revelations	reveal/*revealed*/ revealing/reveals	*revealed*/revealing	x
revenue/revenues	x	x	x
reversal/*reverse*	*reverse*/reversed/ reverses/reversing	reversible/reversing/ irreversible	x
revision/revisions	revise/revised/revises/revising	revised/revisionist	x
revolution/revolutionaries revolutionary/revolutionist/ revolutionists/revolutions	revolutionize/revolutionized/ revolutionizes/revolutionizing	revolutionary	x
rigidities/rigidity	x	*rigid*	rigidly
role/roles	x	x	x
route/routes	*route*/routed/routes/routing	routed/routing	x
scenario/scenarios	x	x	x
schedule/schedules	reschedule/rescheduled/ reschedules/rescheduling *schedule*/scheduled/ schedules/scheduling	scheduled/ scheduling/ rescheduled/ unscheduled	x
schematic/*scheme*/ schemes/schemer	*scheme*/schemed/ schemes/scheming	schematic/scheming	schematically
scope	x	x	x
section	*section*/sectioned/ sectioning/sections	sectioned/sectioning	x
sector/sectors	x	x	x
securities/*security*/ insecurities/insecurity	secure/secures/securing	secure/secured/ insecure	securely
x	seek/seeking/seeks/*sought*	x	x
selection/selections/ selectivity/selector/selectors	*select*/selected/selecting/ selects	*select*/selected/ selective	selectively
sequence/sequences	*sequence*/sequenced/ sequences/sequencing	sequenced/sequential	sequentially
series	x	x	x
sex/sexes/sexism/sexuality	*sex*/sexes	sexual	sexually
shift	*shift*/shifted/shifting/shifts	shifting	x
significance/insignificance	signified/signifies/signify/ signifying	*significant*/ insignificant	significantly/ insignificantly
similarities/similarity	x	*similar*/dissimilar	similarly
simulation	simulate/simulated/ simulates/simulating	simulated	x
site/sites	*site*	x	x
x	x	*so-called*	x
sole	x	sole	*solely*
x	x	x	*somewhat*

source	*source*/sourced/sources/ sourcing	x	x
specification/specifications/ specificity/specifics	x	*specific*	specifically
x	*specified*/specifies/ specify/specifying	specifiable/*specified*/ unspecified	x
sphere/spheres	x	spherical	spherically
stability/stabilization/ instability	stabilize/stabilized/ stabilizes/stabilizing	stable/stabilized/ stabilizing/ unstable	x
statistic/*statistics* statistician/statisticians	x	statistical	statistically
status	x	*status*	x
x	x	*straightforward*	x
strategist/strategists *strategies*/strategy	x	strategic	strategically
stress/stresses	*stress*/stressed/ stresses/stressing	stressed/stressful/ unstressed	x
structure/structures	*structure*/structured/ structures/structuring/ restructure/restructured/ restructures/restructuring	structured/structural/ restructured/ unstructured	structurally
style/*styles*	style/styled/*styles*/styling/ stylize/stylized/stylizes/ stylizing	styled/stylish/ stylistic/stylized	x
submission/submissions	submit/*submitted*/ submitting/submits	*submitted*	x
subordinate/subordinates subordination	subordinate/subordinates	*subordinate* subordinaing	x
x	x	*subsequent*	subsequently
subsidies/subsidy/ *subsidiary*	subsidize/subsidized/ subsidizes/subsidizing	subsidized/*subsidiary*	x
substitute/*substitution*	substitute/substituted/ substitutes/substituting	substitute/substituted	x
succession/successions successor/successors	x	*successive*	successively
sufficiency	x	*sufficient*/insufficient	sufficiently/ insufficiently
sum/sums/summation	*sum*/summed/summing/sums	sum	x
summaries/*summary*/ summarization/ summarizations	summarize/summarized/ summarizes/summarizing	summarized/ summarizing	x
supplement	supplement/supplemented/ supplementing/supplements	*supplementary*	x
survey/surveyor	*survey*/surveyed/ surveying/surveys	surveyed/surveying	x
survival/survivor/ survivors	*survive*/survived/ survives/surviving	surviving	x
suspension	suspend/*suspended*/ suspending/suspends	*suspended*	x
sustainability/sustenance	sustain/sustained/ sustaining/sustains	*sustainable*/sustained/ sustaining/ unsustainable	x

symbol/symbolism/ symbols	symbolize/symbolized/ symbolizes/symbolizing	*symbolic*	symbolically
tape/*tapes*	tape/taped/*tapes*/taping	x	x
target	*target*/targeted/ targeting/targets	targeted	x
task/tasks	*task*/tasks	x	x
team/teams	*team*/teamed/teaming/teams	x	x
x	x	technical	technically
technique/*techniques*	x	x	x
technology	x	technological	technologically
x	x	*temporary*	temporarily
tense/*tension*/tensions	tense	tense/tenser/tensest	tensely
terminal/terminals/ *termination*/terminations	terminate/terminated/ terminates/terminating	terminal/terminated/ terminating	x
text/texts	txt/txted/texting/texts	textual	x
theme/themes	x	thematic	thematically
theories/*theory*/ theorist/theorists	x	theoretical	theoretically
x	x	x	*thereby*
theses/*thesis*	x	x	x
topic/topics	x	topical	x
trace	*trace*/traced/traces/tracing	traceable/tracing	x
tradition/traditions/ traditionalist	x	*traditional*/ nontraditional	traditionally
transfer/transferal/ transference	*transfer*/transferred/ transferring/transfers	transferable/ transferred/ transferring	x
transformation/ transformations	transform/transformed/ transforming/transforms	transformed/ transforming/ transformative	x
transit/*transition*/ transitions	transit/transited/transiting/ transits/*transition*/transitions	transiting/ transitional/ transitory	x
transmission/transmissions	transmit/transmitted/ transmitting/transmits	transmitted/ transmitting	x
transport/transports/ transportation/ transporter/transporters	*transport*/transported/ transporting/transports	transported	x
trend/trends	x	x	x
trigger/triggers	*trigger*/triggered/ triggering/triggers	x	x
ultimate	x	ultimate	*ultimately*
x	*undergo*/undergoes/ undergoing/ undergone/underwent	x	x
underlay	underlay/underlie/underlies/ *underlying*	underlying	x
undertaking	undertake/*undertaken*/ undertakes/undertaking/ undertook	x	x
uniform/uniformity	x	*uniform*	uniformly

unification	*unified*/unifies/unify/unifying	*unified*/unifying	x
uniqueness	x	*unique*	uniquely
utility/utilization/ utilizer/utilizers	utilize/utilized/ utilizes/utilizing	x	x
invalidity/validation/ *validity*	validate/validated/validating/ invalidate	valid	validly
variable/*variables*/ variance/variant/variants variation/variations	varied/varies/ vary/varying	variable/variant/ varied/ varying/invariable	variably/invariably
vehicle/vehicles	x	x	x
version/versions	x	x	x
violation/violations	violate/violated/violates/ violating	violated/violating	x
x	x	virtual	*virtually*
visibility/invisibility	x	*visible*/invisible	visibly
vision/visions	x	x	x
visualization	visualize/visualized/ visualizes/visualizing	*visual*/visualized	visually
volume/volumes/vol	x	x	x
volunteer/volunteers	volunteer/volunteered/ volunteering/volunteers	*voluntary*/ volunteered/ volunteering	voluntarily
welfare	x	x	x
x	x	*widespread*	x

Preposition	Conjunction	Pronoun
x	*assuming*	x
despite	x	x
excluding	x	x
notwithstanding	x	x
plus	*plus*	x
via	x	x
x	*whereas*	x
x	x	*whereby*

Credits

Page 1 image from Yonsei University Press.

Page 4 image from Limb Regeneration: Not Just for X-Men Anymore. 26 May 2006. Medgadget: Internet Journal of Emerging Medical Technologies. http://www.medgadget.com/archives/2006/05/limb_regenerati.html.

Page 17 image Yonsei University Press.

Page 18 image Yonsei University Press.

Page 19 image Yonsei University Press.

Pages 27, 28, 29, 40 and 41 images are in the public domain. NASA copyright policy states that "NASA material is not protected by copyright unless noted." nasa.gov

Information and map for chapter 4 reading, Ecoregions of Korea, from Olson, DM, E Dinerstein, ED Wikramanayake, ND Burgess, GVN Powell, EC Underwood, JA D'amico, I Itoua, HE Strand, JC Morrison, CJ Loucks, TF Allnutt, TH Ricketts, Y Kura, JF Lamoreux, WW Wettengel, P Hedao, and KR Kassem. 2001. Terrestrial Ecoregions of the World: A New Map of Life on Earth. BioScience51. 933-938,

Page 59 image Yonsei University Press.

Page 62 image Yonsei University Press.

Page 75 image Yonsei University Press.

Page 93 image Robert Jeens.

Page 94 image Robert Jeens.

Page 108 image Jason Lim. Philip Jaisohn / Seo Jae Pil: The First Korean-American. Korea Report. 18 April 2008. koreareport2.blogspot.com/2008/04/philip-jais...

Page 109 image Philip Jaisohn. New World Encyclopedia. 2 Apr 2008. http://www.newworldencyclopedia.org/entry/Philip_Jaisohn?oldid=680618.